C000303568

TEARS OF A
HUSBAND

A Husband's journey through
a season of barrenness

By Brian P. Mujuru

COPYRIGHT

Copyright©2020 Brian P. Mujuru. All rights reserved unless otherwise stated, all scriptures quoted are from THE HOLY BIBLE, NEW INTERNATIONAL VERSION®, NIV® Copyright © 1973, 1978, 1984, 2011 by Biblica, Inc.® Used by permission. All rights reserved worldwide.

Scripture quotations marked NKJV are from the Holy Bible, New King James Version®. Copyright © 1982 by Thomas Nelson, Inc. Used by permission. All rights reserved.

Scripture quotations marked KJV are from The Authorized (King James) Version. Rights in the Authorized Version in the United Kingdom are vested in the Crown. Reproduced by permission of the Crown's patentee, Cambridge University Press.

Scripture quotations marked NASB are from the NEW AMERICAN STANDARD BIBLE®, Copyright © 1960, 1962, 1963, 1968, 1971, 1972, 1973, 1975, 1977, 1995 by The Lockman Foundation. Used by permission.

ISBN: 978-1-913663-02-5

CONTENTS

ACKNOWLEDGEMENTS

To God, be the glory, which always belongs to Him. The Author of it all, my beginning and my end. Without Him, the fire within would have remained contained.

To my late father, Silas Maxibaya Mujuru. A great servant and soldier of Christ, Mubvuvi, beloved father and sekuru, ("sekuyu" to my kids). It took me a while to write this but, I want to say I miss you so much. You imparted upon me the gift of serving God and, for that, I am forever grateful. Rest in eternal peace

To my amazing, loving mother, mbuya to my kids, Mrs Greta Mujuru. Thank you for being the mother who never gave up on me through your prayers and crying unto the Lord.

To my two sisters Belinda and Brenda, I thank the Lord for you, for loving me and putting up with my theatrics some times. Love you both.

To the rest of my family and my in-laws thank you for being there and for continuously praying for us. Catherine, Mascline and Rugare thank you for holding my wife down with your prayers.

To the Chief Architect of this project, Vonayi, "Crazy not to Dream" Nyamazana. You are a great visionary. Thank you for the hard work and sleepless nights. To your husband, my friend, my brother Michael Nyamazana thanks for being that Genesis. You guys are blessed of the Lord.

To my Spiritual parents, my father Archbishop Climate and mother Dr Jennifer Wiseman. Words cannot express how the grace God has put on your lives has changed my life. From the first day I got connected, you have loved me as your own, protected me, guided me and allowed me to grow as a son, a man, a father and as a Man of God. Thank you for sowing that fire, hunger and desire in me. The Lord bless you both together with Minister Summer, Minister Climate Jnr, Minister Grace and Minister Sunshine.

To the pride and joy of my life. The evidence and testimony that God can do it. The miracles that defied. Samuel, David and Taome I love you so much. It is you who enabled me to write this book. To my niece, now daughter, Chido. You are blessed forever. Love you guys.

To my beautiful and amazing wife Agatha, my boo, my fashion guru, Mai Sammy, Mai Tatenda, Mai Taome, Mai mwana, Mbuya, Mai Mujuru, Minister Taome, sweetie, baby, so many names and hats I could go on and on but thank you for being an amazing WIFE, LOVER, BEST FRIEND, CONFIDANT, ROCK, COMFORTER and for holding me down (real talk). Thank you for bearing with me and encouraging me to write and talk about us. The fruit of your womb is blessed. Thank you for Samuel, David and Taome. I love you.

And to you who is about to read this story and embark on your journey. May you find what you are searching for. May "Tears of a husband" inspire you to say, "it shall be well with me".

Remain blessed.

FOREWORD

It's my pleasure to introduce to you one of the most amazing books that you will ever have the opportunity to read. In all my years, I've not come across many books like this that leave a profound effect on your life. Pastor Brian's life story carries a lot of weight. Sometimes in life, it takes a real man to come out and talk about the things that no one else is willing to speak of, and this requires a real warrior.

From the cover to the last page of this book, you will experience the epic journey from real emotional struggle to great transformation.

I have known Pastor Brian and have mentored him personally now for almost ten years. As an author of over 50 books, I found my self re-reading his book again and again. And every time I came out stronger both emotionally and physically. As you go through this book, one thing is for sure, that your faith and your emotions will emerge greater and stronger. This book is not just a story, but a formula for a successful life. Read it and enjoy it. This one is a keeper.

RIGHT REV. DR. CLIMATE WISEMAN PHD
THE KINGDOM CHURCH

INTRODUCTION

I had never thought that what was happening could actually happen to me. No, never in a million years. We had tried everything we knew in our power to do, from specialist doctors, spiritualists, different churches, and I could not believe that it was now all coming down to this. So what was different about this, about what was happening now?

I think I may be going ahead of myself. I need to start from the beginning so that you can understand what was going on. This book is my simple but real story of how my life changed when I began to walk with God in the midst of what I thought were insurmountable challenges. I gave my life to Jesus when all hope was lost, when things were messed up and when we were desperately searching for a solution to our problems. My story is about living with the reality of infertility or barrenness; It is about how I, as a man and husband, was baffled by the turn of events in my life because of a challenge that I never saw coming.

Statistics tell us that infertility is a disease affecting one in seven couples. Reading and knowing about it is very different to actually experiencing and living in the midst of it daily. If I may, right at the outset, define the two terms that I will discuss in the book:

Infertility is the inability to conceive naturally. Barrenness is the inability to produce; in other definitions, it is a place of dryness.

These words are used interchangeably and mean "being unproductive". Barrenness is a term mostly used in the Bible, meaning being unable to have children. The causes of barrenness vary, but simply put, the body physically struggles to and cannot produce. The reproductive organs may have some malfunction that makes it difficult or impossible to reproduce. If you want to get spiritual, barrenness can also be as a result of witchcraft or a curse that would have been spun on you.

In the natural or physical realm, our obvious and natural response is to panic when faced by the reality of infertility. In our fear and desperation, we attempt to do all things in our power to get the result we desire. But as believers, we really ought to turn our faith to the Word of God for reassurance and comfort. My faith was tested like never before in this season. All I could see around me at that time was a complete state of dryness, and yet, on the other hand, the Word of God was telling me to hold on to His promises that declare the very opposite; promises of fruitfulness and promises that God had more for me. We know that in the beginning, God gave a mandate to Adam and Eve to go and "Be fruitful, and multiply, and replenish the earth, and subdue it: and have dominion", (Genesis 1:28 NKJV), meaning, to go and reproduce. As Christians, we trust and believe that this is the will of God for us; to be fruitful. Barrenness is not a part of what He has in His plans for our lives.

My journey through that season of barrenness was long, dark and full of despair; there was no hope that we would come to the end of that tunnel. I went through every emotional upheaval you can imagine and more. I was discouraged, disheartened and dejected. As a man, I felt that I was not enough. I felt ashamed and would isolate myself from my friends, my family and my wife. In such a season you ask yourself a lot of "WHY" questions and "WHEN" questions. You question whether there is something wrong with you. Your mind is stretched. Your relationship with your spouse is stretched. Your faith is stretched.

My hope, the only hope I found was in the word of God. And this only happened after I gave my life to Christ and made a decision to walk with God. I discovered that barrenness is spoken about in the Bible, and it is not a situation that is beyond God. The Word of God is full of His vessels that had to deal with the issue of barrenness, from Sarah to Hannah to Rebecca and more. God delivered them all from the state of barrenness and blessed them with the fruit of the womb.

I believe that I went through this season of barrenness for a reason. I believe God was drawing me to Himself and preparing me for His purposes. He dealt with so many of my issues in that season, and in this book, I narrate my journey, as a man and husband. I discuss the challenges that I had to deal with as we journeyed through the state of barrenness to that of abundance. I will take you through the journey that my wife and I walked from the point where we realised that we had a big problem on our hands and how in our panic and desperation we tried to solve the problem. I will also talk about the mixed bag of emotions that attacked me daily as I tried to live and come to terms with what was a challenging reality.

Through it all, God was the great pillar that kept my wife and I going. I share in this book my coping strategies and how we put our faith into action and believed ridiculously for our miracle. "Tears of a husband" is a real-life story, detailing real experiences that I pray you will be able to relate with. It is a story that takes you through a journey of learning to trust and depend on God no matter what you are going through. It is a book that chronicles the emotional journey a husband went through. I pray that you will be blessed as you read this book. This book is about My Life; this is A Husbands Story; This is My Testimony.

CHAPTER ONE

TIME TO FACE MY SELF
...THERE IT IS

Then Jesus said to them plainly, "Lazarus is dead...Now Martha said to Jesus, "Lord if You had been here, my brother would not have died. (John 11:14, 21 NKJV).

I shook my head a little in an attempt to clear it; I was not sure that I'd heard what the Consultant had just said to us. I shook my head again, but this time to force myself back to the present, to focus on what was being said. Our world was turning upside down right in front of us with each word that was being spoken. My wife sat there, dazed, saying nothing and I was trying very hard to make sense of what we'd just heard. I was confused... but how? How could this be? We had believed that this was it; that this time, we would surely hold our baby in our arms.

I had envisioned us living with the pain gone, the shame gone, the years of living in disappointment with a bowed head, I'd thought that all this would now be behind us. Then this. Surely the machines must be broken, mistaken or maybe the nurse did not put enough gel on the probe? Or my wife did not drink enough water for the scan to read properly? My mind was racing, refusing to accept the Consultant's verdict. My heart was beating at a rate that could not be good for it. "What in the world is going on here"? It had to be the machines, what else? Holding tightly onto my wife's hand, we continued to listen, confused, dazed as if in limbo and not knowing what would come next. And still, I held on to that little, tiny glimmer of hope in my heart. I was hoping that there would be a mistake. But it was not to be. It was yet another disappointment.

As men, showing our emotions has always been hard because we are taught to hold it together for the family. Society teaches us to "man up" and not show our emotions. But for how long can one go on for, holding in the emotional turmoil in one's soul? My heart was thudding so loud I thought everyone could hear it. I could feel the pain starting from deep within my belly slowly but surely making its way to my heart. A pain so sharp, set to pierce my heart and break it into tiny pieces. Back home, sitting alone in our bedroom on the bed, holding hands, we broke down and cried.

"I'm so sorry, but we do not see anything in the womb. There is no foetus". The Consultant's words kept echoing in my mind as I tried once more to come to grips with what had just happened. Tears were rolling down my face, as I kept shaking my head in dazed disbelief. My wife was not pregnant? She had never been pregnant for the past three months, even though we had believed that she was. Everything had pointed to the fact that she was pregnant, and the excitement and joy that had filled our lives had been overwhelming. We were complete. It had been such a great relief; we had waited for so many years for this to happen. We had endured years and years of incredible pain, shame and disappointment. And then finally we had believed that this time around God had heard us.

My wife had started experiencing pregnancy like symptoms three months before this hospital visit. Her stomach had started growing as had her breasts. She had cravings for things she'd never had before. I must admit that those late-night trips to the local store drove me crazy sometimes, but the joy of thinking I was going to be a father at last was greater. We were both so ecstatic; we could not believe that finally, it was our turn to celebrate, that our shame would be removed. There would be no more tears in the late nights, no more awkward conversations with people who would innocently ask how many children we have. There was hope, and for me, it was as good as done. We bought all the food she craved, and we had even started buying some maternity clothes for her. That's what belief does to you. It raises your hope and confidence quota. When you are emotionally healthy, your relationship is healthy, everything about your life responds and is happy because your souls are in a good place.

All too soon it was time for the three months check-up. I could still hear the Consultant's voice delivering the news that was such a painful blow, destroying all the hope we'd had. Everything. The hope, the excitement, the anticipation, the joy. It all came crashing down into little pieces in that hospital room. The Consultant said they needed to conduct more tests as they could not see anything. Everything became a blur as he went on to explain the condition that caused my wife to experience these pregnancy-like symptoms. Hours in that room, surrounded by hospital equipment, started to feel like an eternity.

Eventually, my wife had to go to the theatre room to remove the lump that had been growing inside of her. As a man, I had been raised not to show pain, but that day I felt that sharp piercing pain. It was so real it could not be ignored. It hurt me that I was not able to be with her during the procedure, which they described as similar to having an abortion. I was hurt, and in pain, I was confused and in shock. How do you carry on when the world has taught you not to show any emotion, to be strong. How do you deal with your pain and disappointment without feeling and appearing selfish?

I took her home after the procedure, and all I could see was pain, disappointment and lost hope in my wife's eyes. The pain was deep; it was akin to grieving and indeed we had lost something. We had lost that hope, that joy, and we had lost a future. It was something that had been so close, something we could smell, something we nearly tasted, so so near, but only for it to be snatched away from our reach in such a cruel manner. King

Solomon's wise words in the book of Proverbs come to mind and how true, that "Hope delayed makes the heart sick, but desire fulfilled is a tree of life". (Proverbs 13:12 NLT). Another version reads, "Not getting what you want can break your heart, but a wish that comes true is a life-giving tree" (CEV). At that point in our lives, that is exactly how we felt, completely heart sick, utterly crushed, and our hearts broken. And just like King David, I wanted to cry out "I am weary with my crying, My throat is dry, My eyes fail while I Wait for my Lord" (Psalm 69:3 NKJV).

We had to let the families know. Parents from both sides had been so relieved and overjoyed when we initially gave them the long-awaited good news that we were expecting. It was heart-breaking, and we both broke down and cried as we broke the news to them. This was one of the first times that we cried together, sitting on that bed and holding hands. How could this happen? How? Anger rallied with confusion. Confusion rallied with despair. Why had we been denied this happiness? Why had it been snatched away in this cruel manner? We felt cheated. Was this a joke, to play with our minds, play with our lives? What was wrong with us? Even though I was not yet praying or going to church, I found myself calling on God and asking Him why. Where was that God I had called on?

When the ticking bomb, of emotions tightly held in finally explodes, there is no holding it back. But the question is, does it make you any less of a man, any less of a husband? What happens when you hold on and do not express your emotions for what seems to be an eternity? What do you do when everything points to the fact that things are going to be alright and then the mother of all storms suddenly and quickly builds up and creeps up on you, just when you thought the storm was over? Through it all, the emotional turmoil remained inside, unreleased, unshared and waiting to explode. I felt I could not talk to anyone and yet I was falling apart inside. I had to be strong for my wife, but who was being strong for me? Many times as men, we don't want to appear vulnerable or weak, so we continue with the "I can handle this" persona.

I resorted to and found my escape in alcohol; that became my coping strategy every night. I would drink virtually every day and spend most of my time in pubs and clubs trying to run away from the reality around me. The drink numbed the pain. In my drunken stupor, I would temporarily forget the pain of infertility, but the pain would re-emerge when I sobered up. Then the torture would resume in my head. What was wrong with us? Was it me? Was it her? A lot of thoughts and scenarios would flood my mind. Why us? Why me?

My wife was struggling with her anger and pain and finding her own escape. It was a long and dark place, and people did not know what to say to us except for the polite, "it will be ok in God's time". How I hated hearing that statement but I knew they meant well. Time was moving, and I was panicking because my wife and I were not getting any younger. Would it ever happen for us? I never in my whole life thought that anything like this would happen to me. I mean surely things like this did not happen to people like us?

Well, there it is, the realisation of how your life can change and get turned upside down. Your life presented to you in a flash. The reality of what is going on served on a platter for you to see it. You see all the pain and emotions. You are faced with the "what does this mean", and the "what is going on here", questions. In denial, you may want to keep saying "It can never happen to me", but that does not take away the reality. As men, we then tend to start an internal fight with our emotions that take us to breaking point. Should I follow what society, culture and norm have dictated and "man up" or should I ask for help though I feel ashamed and embarrassed? Where is this God I am supposed to trust and believe in?

The Bible tells us that "While He was still speaking, someone came from the ruler of the synagogue's house, saying to him, and "Your daughter is dead. Do not trouble the Teacher." But when Jesus heard it, He answered him, saying, "Do not be afraid; only believe, and she will be made well" (Luke 8:49-50 NKJV).

Jesus told the man not to be afraid even though the situation appeared impossible. Jesus was telling him to put a check, to address and manage his emotions and have faith. There is always hope when you believe and trust in the Lord. Things might appear dead, but with God, all things are possible. His plans, His purpose and His will are good for your life.

CHAPTER 2

PEOPLE LIKE US

"Jonathan, Saul's son, had a son who was lame in his feet. He was five years old when the news about Saul and Jonathan came from Jezreel, and his nurse took him up and fled. And it happened, as she made haste to flee, that he fell and became lame. His name was Mephibosheth" (2Samuel 4:4 NKJV).

The Bible tells of Mephibosheth and how his life changed one day from being a Prince and prospective King, to being a nobody and living in a place called Lodebar. (2 Samuel 9:4). It was a place of dryness, a place of barrenness. Who would have thought that the former King's grandson would live a life of suffering and not one of nobility? His life was once one that fit his status as a Prince. Our lives too, sometimes appear to be normal and things may appear to be moving along nicely until "one day".

I always felt and believed that my life was on course. This kind of problem could not and should not happen to people me, like us. How could it happen to people like us? When what appears to be calamity strikes, shock and denial raise their heads. I remember once when an aunt who was visiting us exclaimed, "What a beautiful home you have, the only thing missing here is the pitter-patter of little feet".

"Oh, here we go again"... I thought. She had a good heart and meant nothing by it, but I couldn't tell you the number of times these sort of remarks were said to us. Statements like these drove the knife even deeper into a wound that was starting to gape wider and deeper.

I had never thought that people like us could suffer such deep problems. It was the sort of thing you heard about; it happened to other people. We had everything going for us. We were a young, hardworking, vibrant and good looking couple. We had it all, the house, the cars, the great careers, and what we thought was a good and modest lifestyle. I mean our life was great, it was amazing. Never in my life, though had I envisioned that I would have to deal with such an issue. I thought that people like us never go through such things as we were going through. Sometimes as men, we never think that infertility or barrenness could happen to you; we think that things automatically go as planned. Nothing can stop or change your dream. You find your soul mate, get married, buy your first home, have kids and yes live happily ever after. When things do not quite go to plan, we find ourselves in a dark place, confused and unable to cope.

Job, in the Bible, states that what he feared and dreaded came upon him in his life (Job 3:25). Was there something that I did? Was it something in my past or childhood? Why was this happening to me? Thinking back, I grew up in what I believed was a normal home life with my parents and two sisters. I met all the expected milestones in my education and childhood. My parents were not wealthy or rich, but they did their best to provide all we needed. I am the eldest child and being a boy; there were high expectations that I would do well. These kind of expectations were nothing out of the ordinary in my culture and community. I felt that I was a regular kind of guy whose life was pretty good. Everything was in order and going to plan with nothing missing and nothing broken. After school, I got a good job with the local, national airline, and my life was on a good, steady roll. My wife and I were just friends back then, but our life journey together was about to start. We were about to embark on this life long journey in search of happiness. I guess all things always work together for good.

Life takes you to extraordinary places for extraordinary seasons. Having moved to the United Kingdom many years later as a young man, I reconnected with my wife and our relationship developed and blossomed from being great friends to dating. Our relationship was not perfect, but we had a connection. My life back then was out of order. I had lost the rails, and you could say that I was a lost cause. I was drinking alcohol heavily and moving with the wrong crowds. I lost many career, schooling and work opportunities because I was wild and irresponsible.

My relationship with my wife suffered as a result of my behaviour. I believe that God must have had plans for us because our relationship was tried in so many different ways. We struggled and many times were at the verge of breaking up. Something stronger than us kept us together, even amid the chaos. We eventually decided to commit to our relationship, and we worked hard at it. I paid lobola, which is the bride price in our culture, and as soon as this happened, I moved to join her in London. I just up and left, leaving everything I owned. We got married at the Registry office; it was a small ceremony with close friends and family, and that was the best thing she ever did for me, and we are still together today. I had decided that my life needed to change and so made my mind up to settle down and started thinking about having children. But life had something else in store for us.

It was in the initial years of our marriage that we discussed having children. We were oblivious to the fact that there was a big problem, and we kept saying that we were not yet ready for children; we had big plans before that could happen. Yes, we had our careers to think about, we wanted to get a house and enjoy life a little before the children came. We were oblivious to the fact that there was an underlying problem that would cause havoc and emotional turmoil in our relationship and life. It was after we hit the fourth and fifth year that we started having concerns that something must be wrong. Looking at us, we were the perfect couple, blessed with everything. Looking at us, you would not know that we were beginning to be tormented by this one thing that was not happening for us. And we had no idea why. I could not understand it. I'd never had to deal with such deep and personal issues in all my life. My life had been normal. My life had not prepared me for such a storm, and I did not know how to fight it. People like us did not have such problems. But we did, and we struggled. Anger, confusion, frustration, depression, shame, humiliation began to build up in my soul. I wanted to talk, but my head told me I could not talk, that it was not manly to talk about feelings. I held everything in, only releasing and expressing some of my frustrations to my wife.

For years I had enjoyed drinking alcohol, but drink had now become an escape from all the chaos and confusion in my head and life. It was my way of coping, and I did not listen to anyone who told me that my drinking was getting out of control. Work was my wife's solace. She found refuge in working long hours. My drinking created arguments, and I accused her of being selfish and never spending time at home. You hear about people having problems but you never in a million years think it could happen to you.

In life, you will come across storms that you had not anticipated. Storms do not discriminate. Problems will come, and it doesn't matter what "kind of people" you are. Storms cannot judge by looks or by status. They just hit. What is crucial for us as a people of God is how we respond when the sorms strike. What matters is how we are prepared and ready when this happens. We were caught unawares, left open and vulnerable to find our way through. Storms come and turn our worlds upside down, bringing with them confusion and panic. Barrenness does not go around looking for you. Infertility does not choose you because of race, because you're poor or rich. Storms come to us all.

Jesus said, in the word of God, that we would all face the storms of life. Life is truly not easy. These storms are many and varied. Abraham faced a storm. Abraham and Sarah waited and waited and had given up. But God is a gracious God, faithful to His word and His promises. "Now the LORD was gracious to Sarah as He had said, and the LORD did for Sarah what He had promised". (Genesis21:1 NIV). It is in the waiting season that we are challenged to keep on trusting God. "Sarah became pregnant and bore a son to Abraham in his old age, at the very time God had promised him" (Genesis21:2 NIV). The Lord had bestowed joy and laughter into their lives.

22

I encourage you if you are going through a storm, if you are facing one, to trust in the Lord and believe what He has said about you. Do not be distracted by the vain realities that you see before you. Hold on to His word. And know that you are never alone, God promises and says, "Don't be afraid. I am with you. Don't tremble with fear. I am your God. I will make you strong, as I protect you with my arm and give you victories" (Isaiah 41:10 CEV). It is only God that can lead you out of that storm. I wish I had known this then. I wish I had been prepared when our storm hit; we could have been saved a whole lot of heartache and pain. Therefore, child of God, when the storm hits, know where to run to and hide. When the storm hits, be prepared to fight because people like us also go through the storms of life.

But as for me, my journey with God had not yet started. My faith did not back my emotional turmoil, but God would soon become a reality in my life.

CHAPTER 3

NO MORE HIDING

"Isaac prayed to the LORD for his wife, because she was unable to conceive children..." (Genesis 25:21 AMP).

There comes a time when your soul tells you that enough is enough. Rebekah must have approached her husband Isaac, distressed, saying that she could not carry on like that anymore. Isaac prayed and made up his mind that something had to be done. The situation could not stay the same anymore; things needed to change. There comes a time when the big elephant in the room has to be confronted, a time to face the awkwardness that causes the soul to endure emotions that torment it daily. Initially, the topic is a no go area with everyone tiptoeing around it but gradually becomes fair game as the years go by. There will always be that one person, though, who is bold and courageous, yet sensitive enough, to ask the question. "When are you going to have children"? "What are you waiting for"?

When you get to this point, there is no more hiding.

"Am I going to die without holding my grandchildren in my arms"? That was my father expressing his pain and disappointment. This question was a long time coming. It was always a waiting game to see who would have the courage to have a conversation about what was going on in our lives. In their minds, they were asking, "Why have you not had children yet", but I guess they could not say it out loud. The reality of our situation was sinking. We could not deny it anymore, and it was now quite obvious to everyone. The usual banter that had gone on before, where friends and family would joke, "come on you guys! It's time to have the little ones" or "What are you waiting for," had now stopped and turned into awkward silences. We could see and feel people's discomfort around us. Family and friends were walking on eggshells around us, avoiding the topic of babies. If there happened to be an opening, we would get the usual encouragement, "it will be well in God's timing". The more I got these questions, the more I felt hopeless and angry. I would blame myself over and over again stating that maybe it was the years of excessive drinking or my previous wild lifestyle that God was punishing me for. I was an emotional wreck yet trying to keep strong for my wife.

Too much time had passed since we had got married, and it was now pretty much obvious to everyone around us that we had a problem. But no one could verbalise the question and ask us what the problem was. People did not know how to ask us. There were periods of high tension between the two of us as we each struggled to deal with this reality. My wife was working long hours at her job, and I guess she hid in her work. As for me, I went to work, went out, drank and slept. It did not remove the problem, but it kept us going. But this was only superficial and for the outside world to see. On the inside, I was hurting badly. I was counting the days, weeks, months and years go by, and with time, that little bit of hope within me would fade away. I was still very guarded; I was not talking to anyone about my problem and the pain I was feeling. I decided that I would bear it out. Beside men don't talk about their emotions.

I remember one particular incident that happened when we attended a family party. There was plenty of free-flowing alcohol, and I remember my wife giving me "the look". That's the "don't you even dare get drunk tonight" look. She knew that when I was drunk, I always embarrassed her. Her advice and "the look" did not stop me from getting drunk that night. During the night I started talking to a certain family member, we were just loud and in his drunken state he started singing about us not having children and that people were waiting for us to have children. In hindsight, it was a funny and hilarious song. I guess it was his way of trying to ask what the problem was. The song did get to me, though. I was drunk, but the hurt penetrated through the haze of alcohol and cut through to the core of my heart. It sobered me up, and I realised the severity of our problem. I needed help; we needed help over this situation. At this point, I had given up and resigned myself to the fact that I would never have children.

We were trying too hard to conceive in that season and at some point, we lost all emotional connection and intimacy as we focused on that one goal, to have a baby. But nothing happened. There is only so much crushing one can take; I struggled to come to terms with the idea that we could not have children. I felt so much pressure because I was the only male child that my parents had, I carried the family name, and my children would be the ones to carry the Mujuru name. I remember thinking to myself that there was no more hiding. Something had to give.

I was tormented and haunted by this reality daily. I did not know where to go for help. I did not and could not talk to anyone about how I felt. The pain was covered up under a mask, and we continued this way, year in and year out. How does one hide their pain at a baby shower? How does one deal with Mother's Day? Father's Day? It is a pain so deep that you only allow it out in the privacy of your home where you can break down and allow the groans of agony to come forth and the tears to flow. No one knew our pain, though many thought they did. Asking again and again and again, Why? When? It is a dark world where you get paranoid, thinking that you are the only ones with such a problem and everyone around you has children or is pregnant. You ask yourself whether you are being punished for something you did in another life? Had God forgotten us? Had He turned His back on us that He could not hear or see our cries?

The Bible tells us that "Then one of the crowd answered and said, "Teacher, I brought You my son, who has a mute spirit. And wherever it seizes him, it throws him down; he foams at the mouth, gnashes his teeth, and becomes rigid. So I spoke to your disciples that they should cast it out, but they could not." Jesus said to him, "If you can believe, all things are possible to him who believes." Immediately the father of the child cried out and said with tears, "Lord, I believe; help my unbelief!" (Mark 9:17-18, 23-24 NKJV). Doubt and lack of faith can creep in as you begin to stop relying on God and start relying on alternatives. But for me, church, God, faith and all things God were not real. If He is God, He should see my problem and move for me. Period!

Couples that struggle with infertility can feel forgotten and isolated even in the church setting. People in or out of church will say hurtful things. You may get some counselling that your infertility is as a result of sin. I would like to believe that their insensitivity in giving such counselling is as a result of lack of knowledge and understanding. They haven't felt the embarrassment of being the only couple in their circle of friends or their family or church without children. They've never nervously waited month after month to find out if this is the month and then get crushed again and again.

Many people live like this for years, living under a mask, hiding their pain and shame. It is torture to the health and well-being of those involved, mentally, emotionally and physically. You become depressed. You may isolate yourself, hiding away from people because you know that they know your issue. You may become paranoid, thinking that people are always talking about your issue. Your life goes on auto, like a robot because you lack motivation and inspiration. The reality of what you feel is shame, embarrassment, rejection. And you grieve every month. You are constantly overwhelmed by feelings of inadequacy. You feel empty, and you feel and believe that you are a failure that is being judged all the time.

I want to encourage you, child of God, that if you are going through a dark place, God has not forgotten you. God is not punishing you. You did nothing that would cause Him to punish you because that is not His nature. He loves you with an everlasting love. (Jeremiah 31:3). He knows you by name even amid your pain and shame; even when people are saying cruel words, He is with you. In His word, He promises never to leave you nor forsake you. (Hebrews 13:5). God remembered Hannah. God heard her groans and gave her the desires of her heart. He will remember you too.

Hold on to your hope. Don't give up on that vision of holding your baby in your arms. Pray. Pray always for God to move in your situation. Believe. Believe always that God, according to His Word, that if I believe with all my heart, something good will come out of it. Nothing is impossible with our God. So when the problem is out, and there is nowhere to hide anymore, this is when you need God to take over. At this point in my life, God was still not an option even though I called out to him. My journey and inability to have children made me run to Him in the end, but there were some pit stops along the way. I decided that there would be no more hiding.

CHAPTER 4

DESPERATE TIMES

"In the morning it happened that David wrote a letter to Joab and sent it by the hand of Uriah. And he wrote in the letter, saying, "Set Uriah in the forefront of the hottest battle, and retreat from him, that he may be struck down and die"
(2 Samuel 11:14-15 NKJV).

David tried and did all he could to solve his problem and get himself out of the mess he had got himself into with Bathsheba. He had made her pregnant and tried his best to make it look like it was her husband who was responsible. In our own lives, when all hope is lost and gone, we may feel trapped and start to believe that we have no choices. Out of a feeling of despair and desperation, we rush out in search for that breakthrough. Fuelled by desire, a vulnerable soul and reignited hope, I believed again and again that there must be a way out for us to bring about the solution we so desired. These were desperate times which called for drastic measures. At this time, God was still not in it.

I remember that growing up; I had this saying that I believed in and firmly held onto. I believed that "if you don't dabble in it, it won't touch you". This belief was especially with regards to issues around witchcraft practices and the existence of ancestral spirits and any powers that they might have. I had no time for such beliefs and did not want anything to do with them. I had no understanding at that time that evil has no respect for such simple sayings and beliefs. When desperate times strike, the very core of your belief system is shaken. You would have tried everything, and at the end of it all you are left with nothing to believe in and hold on to; When you are left empty-handed, you are open to any other suggestions that are presented to you. Desperate times are prone to lead to desperate measures. I want you to think about it for a minute. I want you to take a moment to put things into perspective. What would you do if your beliefs were pushed to the core?

We were going through medical test after medical test. The doctors had suggested that we be medically examined to see if there was anything that needed medical attention. We went through many strenuous, humiliating and invasive procedures. At one point, my wife had to have a laparoscopy and dye test to check that her reproductive organs were in good working condition. The baffling thing was that every test came back fine. There was nothing that was picked up. We changed our diet to a more "healthier one" and adopted a healthy living lifestyle by maintaining fitness through exercise. We were put on many combinations of vitamin tablets to help enhance our chances to conceive. I had to stop drinking alcohol, something I struggled with as this was my escape, the thing that got me to that place of serenity. I remember that I would always find an excuse to drink, and the blame would most often land on me and my drinking as the reason that was stopping us from conceiving. Deep down, we knew it was never about the alcohol.

We were losing hope with every year that went by and eventually the doctors began having conversations with us about In Vitro Fertilisation, (IVF). It was not an easy time or process for us, and the same questions kept coming up - What was wrong with us? Why could we not have any children? Why could the doctors and specialists not explain our inability to have any children? That was a hard pill to swallow from my point of view. It's always your hope that goes, and though you think you are resigned to the fact that you can't have children, hope does tend to rise back up now and again.

All this was taking place as we were reaching the ten-year mark in our marriage and tensions were very high in our home. There was just the two of us, so who do you blame? Whose fault was it? Both sets of parents were concerned, and both were anxious to help. They reasoned that surely if there was nothing that appeared to be wrong medically, then it had to be a spiritual problem. At this point, we were exploring all options. My wife started attending an Apostolic Church where the members dress up in white garments for their services. I refused to attend or participate as I did not understand their practices and had no desire to do so. I would give her unnecessary stress for going there, but she went religiously, Sunday after Sunday. Even though I did not participate in or believe in these practices, at the back of my mind, I was hoping that whatever she was doing would work and that we would get pregnant and have our baby. During services at this church, she would receive prophetic words that she would have a baby. They told her that they could see a baby, but at the end of it all, no baby came.

Throughout all this, I carried on with my carefree, drinking lifestyle. I became very difficult to live with. I was filled with jealous rage and would give Agatha a hard time for coming home late even though I knew that she was coming from work or church. I checked the fuel tank meter to see how much fuel was used so that I could gauge the distance she'd travelled. I would go through her phone at times, feeling that my mind was going crazy. The stress was starting to tear at our marriage.

We continued searching for that elusive baby. I did not know how much more I could take before losing the plot. With each day that went by, the dagger was going deeper and deeper, piercing my soul. We heard about people and churches that could help us. We decided to go to Nigeria to see a Man of God we'd heard about that could help us. But before we completed the travel plans, another opportunity came up that raised our hopes, exciting us. We travelled to Zimbabwe. We felt better going home first, somewhere comfortable and familiar to us. We had heard of a man who was renowned for delivering people from issues such as the one we were struggling with. We were advised that he used both traditional methods as well as prayer. We had nothing to lose at that point. Sometimes when you are caught in that desperate situation, you go through with desperate measures. When you do not know God and you are between a rock and a hard place, anything goes. But throughout this alternative spiritual journey, we found no peace, no solution and no light at the end of the tunnel.

After we flew back to the United Kingdom, many of our friends and family were still reaching out to us, telling us about other traditional options that they knew of and believed could help us. At one point, an old-time friend wanted to introduce us to a man who was reputed as being powerful, and they thought he could help us in our situation. This visit never materialised because both ourselves and our families heard of this man's modus operandi which we were not comfortable with and decided not to go through with it. We felt it was not the right route for us to follow. God was still not a reality for me at this point, and all hope was lost. So, as usual, disappointment was on the menu once again. We still could not get pregnant. Fear of the unknown began to take hold. What was my life going to look like?

People will go to any lengths when in a desperate situation; I learnt this big lesson for myself throughout this journey. We felt so helpless, hopeless and lost. We felt defeated. As a man, I felt the most defeat. In trying to help, people continued trying to introduce us to different religious ministries for spiritual intervention in the hope that things would change and that we would have our breakthrough. When you don't know who God is, when you don't have faith, and you do not have anything to believe in, you are open to anything that comes along. I did not have faith in God then; I did not know Him and had nothing to hold on to at that time. I was sinking into a dark place. Whatever faith we had was surely being tested.

The pressure on me as the man and as the only male child to my parents was real. My two sisters had children one after the other, and we had to be happy for them and congratulate them. My wife's siblings also had children one after the other. It was just us, and that was the reality we had to live with. My hope was crushed. My future was being crushed. The devil was hell-bent on making sure my head would stay bowed down so that I would not walk into my destiny. He was out to steal my joy, kill my purpose and destroy my destiny. And he was winning that battle and winning on all fronts.

Child of God, you have to know who and whose you are and stay grounded in your faith. That way, the distractions and lies of the enemy will not deceive you because you will know how to stand in the time of evil. When you know who you are in Christ, you have hope and reassurance. When you know who you are, you know your value. So I encourage you, child of God, to stand in the authority that is yours and declare who you are. When you know who you are, you can reject the lies of the enemy when they try to invade your thoughts. God will not forsake you, and He is fully aware of your situation, and in the fullness of His time, He will reveal the solutions to your issue.

You are, " a chosen people, a royal priesthood, a holy nation, God's special possession that you may declare the praises of him who called you out of darkness into his wonderful light" (1 Peter 2:9 NIV). And once you know who you are in God, you begin to feel and act how God created you before the foundation of the earth. You start to declare that: I am a child of God (John 1:12), God loves me (1 John 4:10), I am more than a Conqueror (Romans 8:37), I am accepted (Ephesians 1:6), and I am complete in Jesus Christ, (Colossians 2:10).

I knew about God, having grown up in a household where my father and mother both served God mightily. But I had no idea yet who I was in God and how desperate times often call for that desperate cry to God.

What will you do when you have to make that call....?

CHAPTER 5

WHEN TWO OR MORE COME TOGETHER

When David had finished talking with Saul, Jonathan and David became bound together in close friendship. Jonathan loved David as much as he did his own life. (1Samuel18:1NET).

Sometimes some friendships creep up on you, and it is just what the doctor ordered. God is not limited by time, space or situations. When He has marked you for Himself, He will draw you to Himself. He can work in any situation and any location. Many may have disqualified me, but God had not even started with me yet, as I was soon to find out. He has His angels working on your case day and night. God has placed people to catch you along the way so that you may find your way back to Him. He worked on me even in my worst drunken and difficult state.

God sent light and a sign through someone that I could relate with at that time. We met at work and initially only acknowledged each other by extending casual greetings. With time we exchanged telephone numbers and started having conversations. I soon realised that he loved his drink as much as I did and for me, this was a match made in heaven. My new friend and his family lived about five minutes from our new home in our local town.

We began going out for drinks on Friday nights, and we would talk for hours. I found it easy to talk to my new friend because I knew there would be no judgements or preconceived assumptions. Our friendship grew, and our nights out became a regular thing. Initially, we just discussed general "guy stuff". After a while, we decided that our wives should meet and get to know each other so that when we went out as "boys", they would know we were together. At that time, I was just happy that I had a drinking buddy; I grabbed any excuse for me to drink and drown my sorrows. I wasn't going to church yet at that time or even thinking of going but a seed was being planted in my life. When a seed is sown into the ground, it takes time for nature to take its course. Through this friendship, I slowly, unbeknown to me, began to address the emotional turmoil that had been festering on the inside of me without any outlet.

As we continued our Friday night outings, we gained each other's trust, and this made way for our discussions to go deeper. The heavy drinking remained something I was not willing and ready to admit as being a problem. We would have our drinks and talk, but eventually, we stopped going out and started drinking together at home. We would drink for hours through the night while talking about life. We would lose track of time sometimes drinking until the very early hours of the morning. I remember one early morning, my wife calling to ask where I was. I was still at my friend's house, and it was close to five in the morning. It was a freezing winter morning, and when I rushed out to the car, the windows were all frozen, and I remember hurriedly scrapping the ice off and driving back home in my drunken state.

Thankfully it was only a short drive, and there weren't too many cars at that time of the morning. I was always in my element when I was drinking alcohol, but subconsciously I knew that I was numbing the pain. I had slowly started opening up to my friend about my life and how it was affecting me. I did not want to admit it, but it felt good to release. The pressure cap was easing off even though I still had a long way to go.

I remember it took one question from Mike about children and I broke down, pouring my heart out. I opened up and was able to talk about the years of trying and not being able to have children. In our drunken state, we encouraged each other. Mike was also able to speak to me about the issues his family was facing and his personal struggles. We would drink, talk, laugh, and soon our conversations turned to God. We spoke a lot about faith and how it was easy to talk about but difficult to put into practice. Mike and his family were believing God for a breakthrough in their immigration status, and we believed God for the fruit of the womb. We would go into the word of God and dissect it. Mike loved the topic of faith, still does. He loves the book of Genesis and especially the story of Abraham. I was just a novice in the things of God and usually relied on what I had read and heard about in the past. To my surprise, I found myself being able to hold more in-depth conversations about God and my faith was growing without me knowing.

In life, as a man, you need that outlet to express your feelings. Holding things inside is a recipe for disaster waiting to happen. Mike provided the outlet that I needed at that juncture in my life. I could open up to him about anything, knowing I would not be judged. I could get emotional. I talked about my fears of having to live life without children. I could vent my anger and frustrations and rest assured that it was safe to do so. It's always difficult for men to talk, and I am forever thankful to God for this relationship. It was a shoulder to cry on at a very low and dark time in my life. His struggles, his story, his pain helped me to have courage and hope in my issues.

Many times we would also speak about the complicated relationships we had with our fathers. Both of us did not have happy, healthy relationships with our dads, and it was a relief to find someone to talk to about this. We would talk for hours and conclude that despite the challenging issues we had with them, we still loved and respected them for all that they did for us. Things might be difficult now, but they had sown some seeds of wisdom into us as men and as future fathers.

I did not know it then, but something was being sown in my life. Our friendship was a divine connection. God had set a trap for me to prepare my heart for what was to come. It was in these drunken discussions that my faith began to grow. It was the preparation ground for my journey with God. I started to believe that there could be hope. Remember, I was adamant to my wife that I would never go to church. Well, let's say God is good all the time. I started going to church with Mike at his local church. My wife stopped going to the church she had been going as I was still refusing to go there and she started going with me to Mike's church. My mother was in England at that time, and I remember her, just like it was when I was a child, telling me what to wear for church. It did bring joy to her heart seeing me go to church and she loved Mike for that. It is always important to surround yourself with people who are going to build you, encourage you, pray with you and hold your hand in that time of need.

Mike and his family stood with us. They would always put our problems before their problems. We would go away for weekend retreats, and couples getaways. We would go to each other's homes for meals, and to my surprise, we would always end up praying. Initially, I did not like it, but with time it grew on me, and I would look forward to praying whenever we went to his home. I remember once when Mike and his wife had come to our house, and we had prayed, he threw his Bible down and declared that if God be God, if the God we prayed to was the God in the Bible, then we should have our breakthrough. We should have the blessing of fruitfulness and increase.

He stood on his bible to declare that he was standing on the promises of God for us and that the word of God declared in Isaiah 55:11 "So shall My word be that goes forth from My mouth; It shall not return to Me void, But it shall accomplish what I please, And it shall prosper in the thing for which I sent it". We got connected by our faith. We would hold hands and pray together as friends. We would say in our drunken sessions that both our families would celebrate our breakthroughs together and that meant something to us.

Funny thing though, as always happens with alcohol and drunkenness, we would also have our silly moments. We would dream of winning the lottery and that when we did, we would make sure that the whole world knew. We planned that we would charter a Boeing 707 plane to Zimbabwe just for the two of us. We would have all the other seats removed to make room for our white horses that would accompany us on our journey. These two horses would be our way of celebrating our breakthroughs, spoiling ourselves and showing that we could now do whatever we wanted. The horses would hold our passports in their mouths to present them to the immigration officers on our behalf. That's what alcohol makes you do. There were many other moments like this, but I guess it's good to keep some of those stories to ourselves. Why this story of drunken stupor moments though? I was now laughing again and laughing beyond the pain. Sometimes there are things and people that bring you out of your slumber. The morale of this is to remain connected to them that help birth something out of you.

Today this friend is more than just a friend; he is family; he is my brother. All my family have accepted him as such. There are no family events that will take place without him, and my mother will not hear of it. Today we are both men called by God, Pastors, serving in the House of God. Today we both encourage other people not to give up but to hold on to the promises of God. I thank God for this divine connection and relationship. He has been placed in my life for the long haul.

But still during this time, even though I was now open and receptive to God, I continued drinking alcohol as a way to cope with my pain and thoughts. I was now going to church occasionally but would make excuses when I did not want to attend any services. It was during this time in the wilderness, when I was least expecting it, that God came for me.

Are you ever ready for when God comes for you? I know one thing, though, that my friend was always going to be with me throughout this journey.

CHAPTER 6

THE DAMASCUS EXPERIENCE

"Houses of Glory and Power are needed in every city, region and territory. People will then have the opportunity to encounter God's glory and power. Power and glory should be in the Sanctuary. When people have glory encounters, their lives will be dramatically changed and transformed". (John Eckhardt").

An encounter with God transforms your life forever. We all need that encounter; it's necessary for our growth and our faith. It's essential for our relationship with Him. Jesus came that we may have life and have it abundantly (John 10:10). My journey to attaining an abundant life was about to begin. I remember that in that year my wife and I went to America for a six week holiday. Our flight was in the morning, and I had already started drinking alcohol the previous night with my friend, in preparation for my trip. I used to hate flying and would usually be intoxicated. We went for our holiday, and I drank alcohol every day for the 42 days of that vacation. It was that conspicuous that my wife and family urged me to slow down, but I didn't listen and continued anyway. It was now apparent that I had a drinking problem, but I was in denial. If I stopped the alcohol, how would I cope with the pain, with the disappointment of not having children?

We came back from holiday, and I started experiencing migraine headaches nonstop that caused me to cry out in pain at night. Addiction and pain are a deadly concoction. Your emotions play the sick role so well, wanting that medication called alcohol. Despite all this, I continued to drink, causing tensions with my wife. Our relationship was suffering. Arguments had become par for the course for us, and we were heading slowly but surely towards separation even though neither one of us dared to bring it up.

My journey of true faith started around about this time with my introduction to The Kingdom Church. We were introduced to the church by my sister. She started talking to my wife about it, explaining that many people had received their deliverance and been set free, through this Ministry. She encouraged us to attend their services and, eventually, I was persuaded, albeit very reluctantly. I thought to myself, "here we go again with these churches". I agreed to go to stop my wife and mother nagging me about going to church.

Our first attendance was on a Friday evening, and we had to drive, cutting across Central London, through Friday peak-time traffic rush, to get to where the church was. I was sullen; I was not interested and pretty much did not want to be there. The traffic did not help my mood, and by the time we arrived, I was frustrated. I made sure that my wife and my mom, who was with us, knew of my displeasure. I just wanted to be back home where I could go out drinking with my mates. I planned that as soon as the service was over, we would head back home quickly so that I could still go out. I'd been told that the service would be over by about 9:30 pm and this fell in perfectly with my plans.

I remember that when we got there, we were welcomed warmly by an usher. At the time, I did think that she was rather too friendly with the hugs and smiles, a little over the top. Unnecessary, I thought. I was very judgmental and sceptical about everything that was going on. It was not my kind of scene. I did not engage and now and then mom would nudge me and encourage me to stand up during the service. I kept glancing at the time and wondering where this Bishop was and why he was not coming into the service. Even when he eventually did come in, I continued with the assumptions in my head, putting him in a box with other preachers I had heard about or seen on TV.

It was a chaotic scene for me. As the Bishop was preaching and praying, people were falling, and I thought no, this is fake. He's pushing them down. I was not convinced. The service finished late, much later than what we'd been told and this upset me even further. We were then told that there was another service starting at 3 am which we were encouraged to stay and attend. I did not want to. It was midnight, and 3 am was three hours away. It was cold, and I did not like the place. But my mom and wife convinced me to stay, and I went to sleep in the car as I did not want to be in the church. I remember that it was cold and I would turn the engine on and off to keep warm.

Three O'clock came and so did the 3 am Deliverance Service. I had never seen anything like it in my life. The service started with singing but not me of-course; I believed that it was not cool to sing, so I didn't. Eventually, the Bishop came out, and he started praying for people. Everything within me was resisting and did not want to be there. The Bishop explained what was going to take place. He explained that he would pray and lay hands on people and there would be deliverance that would start to take place. I had no idea what this deliverance he was talking about was. The Bishop began going around the room, praying for people and using oil to anoint them, at the same time encouraging people to keep praying.

I was tired and wanted to go home. It was around 04:30 in the morning, and I was leaning against a pillar watching what was going on. People were falling, screaming and crying. Eventually, Bishop came to where I was standing, he instructed me to lift my hands, and he laid his hands on me. The minute he laid his hands on me, I hit the ground and my body started twitching, then shaking and convulsing uncontrollably. Strangely enough, I had a warm fuzzy feeling coursing through me which weirdly felt like being electrocuted. At that point I had no control whatsoever over my body, I was crying, foaming at the mouth and snort was oozing out of my nose. It felt magical yet confusing. I felt that something was different within me, but I could not put my finger on what, where or how.

My mother was getting worried and kept coming to where I was and calling my name. The Bishop advised her to leave me as I was going through a process of deliverance. There were Pastors around me who were praying for me. Mum came again, and this time she tapped me on the shoulder calling my name "Beee, Beee". This time I came to, confused, looking around me, trying to work out where I was. I had a strong sense of conviction that something had taken place inside of me. I could not work out what but I knew that I needed to come back to this place. The urge was so strong, and I could not explain it.

We came back on the next day hoping for something but not too sure what. Nothing happened to me that night, and that threw me, confusing and disappointing me. So I decided that we should come back again on Sunday. That day I felt the urge to go to the front and dance and to pray, shocking my wife. The Bishop came out and started laying his hands on people and praying for them. He approached me, but before he could even put his hands on me, I fell and started shaking and convulsing uncontrollably again. Bishop continued with his sermon as I was on the floor. I was rolling about following him and grabbing at his legs. Once again, I was crying, foaming at the mouth. I had no control what so ever and yet was aware for most of the time, what was going on. I remained on the floor for over an hour and a half, crying and rolling on that floor and sweating profusely. Throughout the whole service, I remained on the floor. At one stage, I tried getting up, but I staggered and fell back down on the floor. Eventually, I managed to get up and went to my chair to sit down.

My wife went up for prayer, and she also fell and went down. I remember that as she fell, she scratched her leg on a chair in the process. When we left that day, I got home and threw away all the alcohol that was in the house.

All the whisky and beers that I had in the house had to go. My wife was in shock, asking me what was going on. I said to her I thought this is what she'd always wished for and that she should be happy to have me going to church and giving up drinking. I no longer had the urge or craving to drink anymore. The migraines that I had also been experiencing stopped just like that. It was a new season for me, for us.

We still had burning questions within us, me more than my wife, that needed answers. It was a new start for us. From then on, we started attending the church regularly, and we loved it. I fell in love with it. We would get excited about going. I stopped wearing my cool jeans to church and started wearing a suit. I remember that I had this one brown suit which I wore. The Bishop put us on what they called a deliverance programme which was a process of being set free from affliction, from demonic and spiritual holds that limit you. These sessions included prayer and we would also have meetings with the Bishop where he would teach us and counsel us, reassuring us of God's love for us. Bishop prescribed a certain number of days for us to attend the deliverance sessions. He would pray for us, laying hands on us. The whole experience was new and confusing to me, but when you have good, godly people around you to walk you through, it becomes easier.

I found it amazing that God could love someone like me, who had so much baggage. As Bishop continued praying, prophesying and speaking over my life, my faith began to grow. I had gone to Church because my wife and I were seeking a solution to a problem that we had. But instead, I encountered God; we both encountered God. I had grown up in church, going because I was being made to go, but this time I discovered God for myself on a very personal level.

With time, we started to serve in the church. I began to serve directly under the Bishop, eventually being elevated to Chief Armour Bearer as the Arch Deacon. As I served, I began to grow spiritually. Throughout our deliverance sessions Bishop would reassure us that we would have our baby and he would be a boy. We had told him about all the places we'd gone to seeking help, the spiritual healers and the different ministries. During this time, my wife and I were tested financially. I was still a student, and we attended church five times a week, travelling about long distances to get to church. It was challenging financially, but God always provided.

We eventually completed our deliverance prayers programme, and my expectations were high. I had no idea what to expect next. We serve a miracle-working God. When He opens doors, no man will close them. Nothing is impossible with Him. An encounter with God will touch and deal with the inner-most issues of your heart. An encounter with God will transform your life, ushering His light in and banishing all darkness. An encounter with the Lord will fill your heart with excitement and passion for Him. An encounter with Jesus will allow you to be open and receptive to God and His ways. The Bible tells us that "As he journeyed he came near Damascus, and suddenly a light shone around him from heaven" (Acts 9:3 NKJV).

No matter what you are going through, God will always see that glimmer of hope, the little faith, that connection you desire with Him. He will come for you when you least expect, deliver you and let His will be done upon your life. This was my life-changing encounter, my deliverance, my Damascus experience. And even though we still were not pregnant, there was a peace and rejuvenated hope within me. You need to maintain hope against all hope during your challenge.

CHAPTER 7

EMPOWERED

I can do all things, which He has called me to do, through Him who strengthens and empowers me, to fulfill His purpose-I am self-sufficient in Christ's sufficiency; I am ready for anything and equal to anything through Him who infuses me with inner strength and confident peace(Philippians 4:13 AMP).

We have since come to understand that sometimes all it takes is that one encounter with the right connection to take you to your breakthrough or miracle. I was led to church because we were desperate for a solution to our problem; I wasn't looking for God, or to be a regular churchgoer. I was looking for a solution to anything that would give us some hope. But to be honest, for me, it was also to put a stop to the nagging from my wife and mother. I was getting pressure from my mum, my wife and my sister. I was not sure that anything would happen. I also had a fear that it might not work, but on the other hand, I also feared that if I didn't attend this church and give it a go, I would live with the regret of never knowing if it would have worked for us. Ten years is a long time to wait, and we had tried everything and been everywhere to find help. So we went to this church not knowing that this was the divine connection that we needed to take us to the next season of our lives.

In the same way, faith by itself, if it is not accompanied by action, is dead. (James 2:27). When we connected with the Kingdom Church, we went through an intensive programme, digging deep into the word of God and praying. Afterwards, we felt lighter, like something heavy had been lifted off us. We were delivered from whatever had been limiting us from living the life that Christ intended for us. So many things had to be broken off our lives, and through it all, the Man of God would speak the Word of God over us and prophesy that we would have our baby. He prophesied that our firstborn would be a baby boy.

The scripture that we held on to and believed for our miracle was at the tip of our tongues every day. It stated that "and He will love you and bless you and [a]multiply you; He will also bless the fruit of your womb and the fruit of your land, your grain and your new wine and your oil, the increase of your cattle and the offspring of your flock, in the land of which He [b]swore to your fathers to give you. You shall be blessed above all peoples; there shall not be a male or female barren among you or among your livestock. And the Lord will take away from you all sickness, and will afflict you with none of the terrible diseases of Egypt which you have known, but will lay them on all those who hate you" (Deuteronomy 7:13 -15). We came alive again. We felt that we were ready. There was something different about us; we had a zeal for the word of God and His promises. We felt empowered and had a constant hunger and desire for all things God. Our faith was growing, and we were putting it into action. It felt very weird and crazy at first, but we began to trust God more and more. We saw in the Bible that those who often got their miracles did weird and crazy things that were out of the norm.

As we continued to wait and believe for the fruit of the womb, we were given scriptures to confess together every single day — part of what needed to happen between us was to reconnect on an emotional level. We would do everything that needed to be done physically to have children, but it was devoid of emotion. We started praying together, holding hands every night and confessing the word of God over our lives and the situation. We were rebuilding our bond emotionally, physically and spiritually. If one of us were away, we would call each other and pray over the phone.

Each week when we had our session with the man of God we would sow a seed of £7,13 into our situation, coming into agreement with the word of God that we would have the fruit of the womb. (Deuteronomy 7:13). We did not stop at just confessing; We went all out to believe that we would hold our baby. We continued to put our faith into action. At the same time that we were confessing scripture and going to church, I was growing fast in the things of God. My wife also read and concentrated on using Devotional books written by the woman of God, Dr Jennifer Wiseman, books that focused on subjects like marriage, children and pregnancy. We would confess the scriptures in the Devotionals every day. I remember that we were on overdrive with the word of God. We started buying baby clothes as a point of contact for our faith. We took one set to church and would pray for it at the altar and leave it there. We took another set to Edinburgh, which is where the Ministry headquarters of the church is located, and my wife would regularly ask for the Woman of God to pray over the set. We kept another set at our altar at home.

We also listened to a CD called "BABY COMETH" by the Woman of God. We listened to this CD daily and would leave it to play in the house or overnight as we went to sleep. The purpose of the CD is to encourage women who are believing for the fruit of the womb, to believe God for their miracle and to build up their faith. It had beautiful, soothing music in the background and the sound of a baby crying. The Woman of God would then start praying and reciting scripture, going through prayer points to encourage and build faith. It empowered and encouraged us to start to envision our baby as we heard the sound of the baby resounding through our home, to see ourselves holding our baby , and we believed that it was done. Hearing the sound of the baby was a faith extender. The sound was released throughout our home. The power of the Word of God was released into our hearts and spirits as well as into the atmosphere. We would play the CD on repeat throughout the night. We were putting our faith into action 100%.

I also remember that at around the same time, there was a woman in the church who was also believing God for the fruit of the womb and had bought a baby vest as a faith extender. She took the garment to the Bishop who prayed daily, speaking the word of God over it and declaring that her baby would come. This lady was, in time, blessed with a son, and she came to church to give her testimony with her baby in her arms. The Bishop took the vest and asked the church if there was anyone who was believing for the fruit of the womb, and as he did so, he tossed the vest out to the congregation. My wife ran to catch it. After that, she carried that vest with her everywhere, in her handbag, praying over it and calling forth her breakthrough. Our journey was by no means easy, but we continued believing and pushing through. Many a time I wondered if our breakthrough would come at all. What if it did not? Then what? These were difficult questions that I wrestled with all the time.

During yet another Sunday Service, which I have come to believe was the tipping point for us, the Bishop asked if there was anyone in the service who was believing for the fruit of the womb and if so, to run to the front. My wife leapt up and ran to the front. She was the first one at the altar with two other women behind her. He prayed for the three women and prophesied that "This time next year you will have your baby". My wife received the word, believed it and sowed a seed to seal it. We believed so much in God, we believed His word, and we sowed seeds unto to Him.

Beloved, the word tells us to pray without ceasing. It tells us to persist in prayer. And to believe that what you believe for will come to pass. We know that faith without action is dead; we had to fight and push our faith through. It's easy to give up when you do not see results, it's easy to say, "well I tried" and move on to something else, but Child of God, I am here to say that don't give up on your miracle. Sorrow may last for a night, but your joy will surely come. Pray, I say. Believe I say. And keep pushing. The season I spent learning to know God again was the most amazing time. I learnt to trust God, even when things did not seem possible. The word of God empowered me to push for those promises of God.

CHAPTER 8

THE PROPHETIC IN YOU

As believers, we believe that we are created in the image of God. We move and breathe and have our being in Him. God is the Creator of ALL things. He spoke, and things became. As He creates, so can we. We have the power to speak things into being. We have the power to prophesy life into dead situations. All that He asks is that we have faith as a mustard seed. Faith to believe that those things we believe in, can and will come to pass. "Truly I tell you, if anyone says to this mountain, 'Go, throw yourself into the sea,' and does not doubt in their heart but believes that what they say will happen, it will be done for them. (Mark 11:23 NIV).

You have a God-given ability in you to speak life and to speak breakthrough into your situation. Speak it. Speak to it and believe it. There is a power vested in you enough to cause a change in the atmosphere. You have dominion and power and authority to shift things in the atmosphere. Then God said, "Let Us make man in Our image, according to Our likeness; let them have dominion over the fish of the sea, over the birds of the air, and over the cattle, over all the earth and over every creeping thing that creeps on the earth" (Genesis 1:26 NKJV).

To Adam and Eve, after blessing them, God said, "Be fruitful and increase in number; fill the earth and subdue it. Rule over the fish in the sea and the birds in the sky and over every living creature that moves on the ground". (Genesis 1:28 NIV).

God empowered us and gave us the ability to prosper and have success in all that we do. From the beginning, it was so, and we need by faith to believe that it remains so. "The LORD God formed out of the ground every living animal of the field and every bird of the air. He brought them to the man to see what he would name them, and whatever the man called each living creature, that was its name. (Genesis 2:19 NET).

So the man named all the animals, the birds of the air, and the living creatures of the field, but for Adam no companion who corresponded to him was found". (Genesis2:20 NET). The prophetic was sown into man by God from the very beginning. Whatever Man spoke, God said it was so. Whatever you speak henceforth, let it be so. Let the Word of God empower you.

Death and life are in the power of the tongue, And those who love it will eat its fruit. (Proverbs 18:21 NKJV). The one who guards his mouth and his tongue keeps his life from troubles. (Proverbs 21:23 NET). James 3 talks and teaches about the power of the tongue. Once you understand the prophetic power of the word of God and begin to speak into your situation, that confession will begin to bring forth manifestation. Jesus also said, "Truly I tell you, if anyone says to this mountain, 'Go, throw yourself into the sea,' and does not doubt in their heart but believes that what they say will happen, it will be done for them. (Mark 11:23 NIV).

My wife and I decided to speak prophetically into our situation, using the powerful word of God. Just like Hannah did, we also entered into a contract with God. We put His word to the test and decided to stand on it without wavering. Sometimes when crisis strikes, you have to go before God with a faith that is almost ridiculous to the ordinary man. It was not easy, but we stood firm on His word.

Below is the prophetic contract we made with God. We printed a copy and signed both our signatures and confessed and prophesied into our lives daily as we prayed together.

Brian and Agatha's case before the Lord:

- I shall put God in remembrance of his promises; I shall keep not silent. I shall give Him no rest until it comes to pass according to Isaiah 62:6-7.

- I declare and decree that what I open no man can shut, What I shut no man can open in the name of Jesus as in Revelation 3:7.

- And God will make all grace, every favour and all earthly blessings come to me in abundance, so that I may always and under all circumstances and whatever the need, I shall be self-sufficient possessing enough to require no aid or support and will be furnished in abundance for every good work and charitable donation (I have more than enough) as in 2Corinthians 9:8.

- You let men ride over my head, I went through fire and water, but you brought me to a place of abundance as in Psalm 66:12

- The Lord, the God of my fathers, will increase me a thousand times and bless me as he has promised as in Deuteronomy 1:11

- In everything that I do, I will reap a hundredfold return because the Lord has blessed me. (Genesis 26:12)

- And the ark of the Lord continued in the house of Obed–Edom the Gittite three months: and the Lord blessed Obed–Edom, and all his household. My household shall be blessed according to 2 Samuel 6:11.

- We shall receive a hundredfold return in this present age and in the age to come because of our commitment to the gospel according to Mark 10:29-30.

For God You said:

- We shall be fruitful, and we shall multiply. (Genesis 1:28)

- Our children shall be Might in the land of their dwelling. (Psalm112:2)

- Our children are a heritage and blessing from you God and our offspring a reward and gift from you. (Psalm 127:3)

- Isaac prayed to you, Lord on behalf of his wife because she was childless. Lord you answered his prayer, and his wife Rebekah became pregnant. (Genesis 25:21)

- And none of us will miscarry or be barren in our land. You will give us a full life span. (Exodus 23:26)

- My wife will be like a fruitful vine within my house; my children will be like olive shoots around my table. We shall live to see our children's children, and there shall be peace on Israel. (Psalm 128:3-6)

- When the time comes for Agatha to give birth, there will be twins, a boy and a girl in her womb. (Genesis 25:24)

- No weapon that is formed against me shall prosper, and every tongue that shall rise against me in judgment shall be condemned. (Isaiah 54:17)

- No longer will violence be heard in my land, no more ruin, no more destruction, no more devastation within my household and my families household, but I will call my walls Salvation and my gates Praise. (Isaiah 60:18)

- And He will love us, and bless us, and multiply us. He will also bless the fruit of our womb, and the fruit of our land, the fruit of our grain, and the fruit of our wine, and the fruit of our oil, the increase in our children, love, joy, peace, marriage, finances, money, wealth, our faith, our blessings, our power, our authority, our family relationship, our relationship with God, our relationship with Jesus, our relationship with the Holy Spirit, the Gifts of the Holy Spirit, the fruits of the Holy Spirit and all the positive aspects of our lives, in the land in which he swore to our fathers to give to us. We shall be blessed above all people, and there shall not be male or female barren among us, among our children, their children and the generation to come. And the Lord will take away from us all sicknesses, lack, barrenness and poverty. He will afflict us with none of the terrible diseases and misfortunes of Egypt which we have known, but he will afflict them on all those who hate us in the name of Jesus. (Deuteronomy7:13-15).

"Lord as we have presented our case and promises to you, we believe them, we receive them, we claim them, we keep them, we have been granted them, the physical manifestation of your blessing oh Lord, which you have prepared for us before the foundation of this world. We thank you and give you all the glory and promise to dedicate our children to you, Lord for the rest of their lives. Amen".

As we continued to grow in the Lord, we began to trust Him more and more. We believed that it would come to pass though it seemed impossible at times. We confessed and declared these scriptures every day without fail, tired or not tired, when we felt like it and when we did not feel like it. We decided to come together and confess the word of God in agreement. There is power when you stand together in agreement for a common purpose. Begin to see manifestation as you confess the word of God. There is a prophetic in you to birth your breakthrough.

CHAPTER 9

"THE DIAMOND IN THE ROUGH."

"These things says He who is holy, He who is true, "He who has the key of David, He who opens and no one shuts, and shuts and no one opens" (Revelation 3:7 NKJV).

God will move you from infertility to abundance when His time is right. He makes "everything beautiful in its time." (Ecclesiastes 3:11 NIV). He truly does.

We were so engrossed in our newfound faith; We were praying, confessing and declaring God's Word over our lives. We started eating right. We wanted everything to be in order, the emotional, the physical and the spiritual, doing our part to create the right environment for our miracle to manifest. Our expectation created the atmosphere for our miracle. Then bam!.... it happened! My wife missed her monthly period! My heart jumped straight to my mouth, then pounded so hard. We got so excited and I rushed out to the local supermarket to buy a pregnancy kit. We did the test, but it was a false alarm. She was not pregnant. The disappointment in both our eyes was so evident, and we could feel doubt and lost hope starting to creep back into our hearts once more. "God, I have given my life to you, please do it for us because I cannot go on like this anymore". That was my heart crying out to God.

Then it happened the following month again! My wife said that she did not feel right. Again I rushed out for the pregnancy kit, my heart pounding as I drove there and back, praying the whole time that God would do it for us this time. It's funny how we never seemed to have the pregnancy kit when we needed one. This time I made sure I went into the bathroom with her. The atmosphere was so tense with a mixture of both excitement and uncertainty as we did the test once again. I know that I could hear my heart thudding in my chest and at that point, it seemed as if everything went into slow motion. There were mixed emotions of anxiety and excitement, at the same time praying and praying that please God let it be so this time. Please, God.

We closed our eyes and prayed. We then opened them to check what the result was, but there was a very faint line which wasn't very clear at all, and we did not dare get excited just then. We decided to do another test to get a more definite result and… this time there was a very distinct line! It was surreal; we could not believe it; we jumped and cried and screamed, but also trying not to make too much noise in the bathroom because my mother in law was around. We prayed, kissed and hugged each other so tight. This was it! It had happened for us…at last! I couldn't wait to tell Bishop, and so I went outside and got into the car to call him.

Bishop shouted in his excitement and exclaimed: "I told you God would do it for you"! He prayed, and the power of God hit me right there in the car, leaving me shaking and convulsing. Bishop advised us to use wisdom and not to say anything to anyone for the first three months. That was one of the hardest things we'd ever had to do. Keeping quiet when everything within us wanted to scream out to the world: "We are pregnant"! The pregnancy changed everything for us. We had a secret. It was our very own secret, and it drew us closer. We continued praying and confessing the word during those three months.

The three months went by quickly, but our excitement soon turned into fear and worry once again. It was time for the three months scan at the hospital to check that the pregnancy was going well and that the foetus was growing. We remembered the nightmare of the year when we thought my wife was pregnant, and it had turned out that she was not pregnant after all. It felt like "deja vu". We went to the hospital, and the wait was like an eternity. Our hearts were pounding as we prayed, holding hands tightly in the waiting area.

"Agatha you're next, hope you've drunk enough water," said the nurse as she led us to the side room for the scan. At this point, I couldn't even hear her voice. The thudding in my chest was deafening. She prepared my wife and applied the gel to her stomach. My heart was now beating so fast, and my hands were clammy. "There you are," the nurse said, "here take a look, everything seems fine." She turned the monitor for me to see, "your baby appears to be growing well," she said as she continued to play around with the probe on my wife's stomach. What a relief! Talk about your faith being tested over and over again! We got the pictures of the baby scan and went home. We phoned our Bishop and his wife and told them the good news about the dating scan and advised them of the estimated date of delivery.

After the three month scan, we were able to tell our families and friends. Both sets of parents broke down and cried. It was very emotional for everyone. So many people had walked this difficult journey with us and believed with us. There was both tears and laughter when we told them the news. Life had to go on, but this time there was so much excitement and anticipation. We continued with our new lifestyle and praying together. We went for another scan during the pregnancy to reveal the sex of the baby, and just like the Bishop had spoken, it came to pass. We were having a baby boy! It was turning out to be a great year. The pregnancy went well, but the baby was late and had to be induced.

On the day of the birth, my wife was allocated a midwife who was as excited as we were but her shift ended before the baby came. She handed over to another midwife and decided to stay so that she could be present for the birth. What we were to find out later was that the one who took over was a Christian...we were in awe at the way that God orchestrates the events of our lives. Our baby was to have a Christian Midwife! When my son was born, it was the biggest miracle of my life. I cried tears of joy nonstop. When he was placed in my arms, I knelt, lifting him to God with tears running down my face. I prayed, thanking God for our son and dedicated him to God. The midwife was shouting "AMEN" in the background! Mother and baby were soon discharged, and as soon as we got home, I knelt again before entering the house, lifted my son and gave God the glory. We asked the man of God, the Bishop, to name our son. And so he was named Samuel, after the Prophet of God in the bible. We then called him Taona, a Shona name from Zimbabwe meaning "we have seen". Samuel's birth was an experience that would forever be etched in our hearts and minds. It was the most amazing and miraculous thing to happen to us, and to God be all the glory. Samuel was the most spoilt baby ever, the most waited for, and everyone was willing to help and do anything for him. We did not stop going to church just because our prayers had been answered. We continued to serve in the House of God. What we have learnt is that when you trust God, miracles happen.

"Son, how many children do you want"? The question came as I was with Bishop one day, serving under him. I answered that whatever God would permit, but Bishop said you must understand that whatsoever God opens, no man can shut and God will give you more and more as you desire. He again asked, "how many children do you want"? I then responded that we would love to have three or four. "So shall it be", declared the man of God. "God has opened the door so go and have the children". I received the word and sealed it with a seed. I am a great believer in seed sowing. I believe that seeds speak into the future.

My wife was off work for over a year, looking after Samuel. Her mum was around to help out. Eventually, my wife had to go back to work. After a while, when we felt we were ready, we went back to the man of God and told him we now believed God for a daughter. We were excited, and we sowed a seed into this second pregnancy. We did the same as before, praying together and confessing the word of God over our lives. We made sure that we were feeding well spiritually, emotionally and physically. It was very exciting knowing that we had come from a position of barrenness to one where we could conceive at will. The three months rule still prevailed after we conceived our second baby. We believed God for a daughter but the man of God this time did not commit and only smiled saying "whatever God blesses you with, we receive". It was like he already knew that it was not going to be a girl.

The baby was born, and it was another boy! He was late, and an emergency caesarean had to be performed because he had pood in the womb, (meconium), and they did not want the risk of the baby breathing in or choking on his faeces. When he was born, I went on my knees again and thanked God for him and dedicated him back to God. We asked the man of God, as we had done with Samuel, to name the new baby. He was named David, after King David in the Bible. And we gave him a Shona name, Tatenda, meaning "we are thankful". With both babies, when I got home, I would kneel at the door and give thanks to God for their lives. This season of our lives was exciting. The family was buzzing. Our friends were buzzing. The church was abuzz with excitement, saying that we were now populating the Sunday School single-handedly.

We were not done yet. Our daughter was conceived soon after David. The baby was overdue, and the Consultants had to induce birth. The progress was slow. Eventually, we were informed that the baby was in distress and had wrapped herself around the umbilical code. I remember the midwife getting on the bed with my wife lying there, holding the baby's head so that it would not go down and get strangled. All of a sudden, there was a hive of activity as consultants and paediatricians rushed in, making the decision that my wife should go into theatre straight away. She was wheeled out on her bed. I was not allowed to go in with her, and I went into a panic. I called Bishop, who prayed and reassured me that all would be well.

The wait outside was agony, but I continued praying. I was genuinely afraid. Eventually, a nurse came out, and I could swear that my heart stopped at that moment. She advised me that I was the proud father of a baby girl, and at that, I broke down right there and cried. I was on the floor in the corridor holding her hand crying and shouting "thank you, Jesus". I knelt again and prayed, thanking God for the beautiful gift that was my daughter. Holding my daughter and my wife when they came out of the theatre was amazing, and I was overwhelmed with so much emotion. There was much crying, tears of joy and tears of gratitude. I knelt, lifted my daughter to God and thanked Him for her, dedicating her to Him. As with her brothers, we asked the man of God to name her. He went into the book of Job and chose one of the names from the daughters of Job, Jemimah. We called her "Taome", a name I had carried in my heart for many years to give to my daughter when I had her. Now I know better, that it was the vision of having a daughter that I had carried in my heart.

"Write the vision, And make it plain on tablets, That he may run who reads it. For the vision is yet for an appointed time; But at the end, it will speak, and it will not lie. Though it tarries, wait for it; Because it will surely come, It will not tarry"(Habakkuk 2:2-3 NKJV). It was in 2003, and we were newly married with no plans of having children. At the time, I worked for an agency that sent me to work at a Day Care Centre for Older Adults. Two ladies of Jamaican descent used to attend the Centre, one very feisty and the other very calm and collected. One day the calm and collected lady was talking about her granddaughter, who was celebrating her birthday that day, and she mentioned the granddaughter's name, which caught my attention. It was a beautiful name, and I was intrigued. It was "Taome". I asked her what it meant, and she said: "it means the apple of my eye". I fell in love with the name right there and then and asked the lady for permission to use the name for I had my daughter.

I held that name in my heart for all the years that we believed for the fruit of the womb. God reminded me that it was at that point when I took the name for my daughter's in 2003, that initiated the inception of the conception in my mind. It was the birth of the vision for our children. In my ignorance, I had birthed the vision for the birth of my children. I had declared that

I would have a daughter, and I held on to that name for over 12 years. In the spiritual realm, we had set that we would have a daughter. Our hope was set. God works all things to work together for us. He is the greatest Choreographer of our lives. His word in Jeremiah 29:11 says: "For I know the plans I have for you,… plans to prosper you and not to harm you, plans to give you hope and a future". As long as the vision is there, it will come to pass. Do not give up on your vision. Hold on to it for in the end, the vision will speak.

God can move you from a place of lack to one of abundance as He wills. He makes everything beautiful in its time. He took us from a place of infertility to one of fruitfulness. Whatever it is that you believe for, God can move in your situation. There was nothing special about us, we were just ordinary people, and God moved in our case. We are forever thankful for our three miracles, our blessings Samuel, David and Jemimah. What a faithful God. It was also one of my most fervent prayers that my parents would see and hold my children in their lifetime, and I thank God that my father got to hold all my children before he was promoted to glory. Today it's all about blue, blue, pink — the diamond in the rough.

CHAPTER 10

WAITING ON THE FRUIT OF THE WOMB

"Behold, I am the LORD, the God of all flesh. Is there anything too hard for Me? (Jeremiah 32:27 NKJV)

When you are in that waiting room:

- You deal with the mixed bag of emotions

- You deal with family and friends

- You have to make up your mind about whether or not to believe God

- You have to make up your mind about what happens next

Waiting for anything in life happens to be one of the things that we do not excel in. Everyone is in such a hurry and demands results or answers "now". So having to wait for nearly ten years for something we desperately desired was a test that was very challenging for me. I believe that we were stretched and tried in every which way, but now I can stand and say "the grace of God" is indeed sufficient. Growing up, I never really wanted to go to church. The minute I was old enough I stopped going, deciding that it was not for me. I had no interest whatsoever in it. But the one thing that I do know now is that those early years of my going to church set a firm foundation of Christ in my life whether I wanted it to or not. It was that foundation that carried and sustained me in the wilderness season. I was a child of God, and the foundations laid by my parents influenced my life directly and indirectly. I can see the word of God coming to pass in my life that says "Train up a child in the way he should go, And when he is old, he will not depart from it". (Proverbs 22:6 NKJV).

When I chose to move away from God, I stepped into a wilderness season, one that lacked direction and was filled with confusion. It was a time when I had no cares in the world, believing that my life was fine until something hit me hard, and I realised that all was not well. I hadn't walked with God for decades when we hit rock bottom and were desperate for help. My immediate response was acute frustration, anger, playing the blame game and pointing fingers. As far as I was concerned, it wasn't my fault; it had to be her. I did things that distanced me from my wife. And because I did not believe in God, I believed everything the doctors said. I did not know anything else. My faith was in the medical field and other alternative solutions that were on offer.

That season was depressing and even embarrassing for me as a man, but I could not show or share these feelings. We tried to get solutions through the medical field. We had so many tests, diet changes, and so much advice and guidance from friends, family and other sources. Any guidance, advice or encouragement leaning towards God would fall on deaf ears on my part. My choice was to believe what the doctors said.

What did not help, that we found difficult to deal with was being around people who were pregnant and or surrounded by children. It could not be avoided all the time, but we still found it to be a bit challenging. It was hard being around people who would avoid the subject of our infertility and pretend that all was fine, avoiding the elephant in the room. We went through uncomfortable, awkward, unbearable and distressing situations before we got to our breakthrough. But there came a time when we had to confront the elephant in the room with the word of God. It was time to get out of our comfort zone and work through the pain.

When my life turned around, and I started walking with the Lord, my newfound faith kept me going and uplifted. I still was frustrated, and I still had questions and kept asking "when Lord"? But now I knew to lean on and put my trust in God. I believed that He would move in my situation. We now had hope, and our hope was firmly anchored in Christ. My life and focus changed and the Word of God was at work inside of me, and it began to wipe away the anger and frustration. I learnt to confess the scriptures for myself. My life started to change and to have meaning:

- I started going to church regularly

- I stopped drinking alcohol straight away, and this cleared my head

- I lost those people that I had considered to be my friends. They dropped off because they could not understand the change in me

- I started spending more time with my wife and less time in the clubs

In this season of our lives, we had to find ways to cope as we waited for our breakthrough. But how does one cope when what you see around you every day is barrenness? I now know that it is of paramount importance to have a firm foundation in the things of God. The Word of God was becoming so entrenched in me that my faith was being built up. It is necessary to hear the word of God often, and we are taught this in Romans 10:17 that "faith comes by hearing, and hearing by the word of God". (NKJV).

When you are built on the solid foundation of the Word of God, you have no choice but to grow and flourish. We are given an example in the word of God in Mathew 7:24 -27 which says "Anyone who listens to my teaching and follows it is wise, like a person who builds a house on solid rock. Though the rain comes in torrents and the floodwaters rise, and the winds beat against that house, it won't collapse because it is built on bedrock. But anyone who hears my teaching and doesn't obey it is foolish, like a person who builds a house on sand. When the rains and floods come, and the winds beat against that house, it will collapse with a mighty crash." When you are standing on solid ground, you can deal with the storms when they come your way.

This is how we coped during the difficult season of waiting for the fruit of the womb:

- We had to believe that the will of God would prevail. We relied entirely on the word of God

- We went to church and focused on building a strong relationship with God

- We fed on the word of God. We were taught and prophesied over to empower and encourage us

- We called on the name of Jesus

- We had to have a definite conviction that God would do it for us

- We prayed together as a couple every night

- We started a lifestyle of prayer and fasting together as a couple

- We surrounded ourselves with people who were positive and who could join their faith with ours in believing for our breakthrough

- We started to speak more openly with our families.

We started taking care of our bodies. We ate well, and we exercised

We encourage anyone going through this same season to seek medical help and advice. God is the ultimate healer, but it is also wise to seek the medical field to find out what is going on in your bodies. Try not to isolate yourselves; It's essential to have family and friends around to support and encourage you.

Love each other; You are in the situation together. Stay together and work together in unity, and you will see things starting to change and work for you. There is power in agreement. The enemy seeks to bring division between you to weaken your bond so that you start arguing and blaming each other.

CHAPTER 11

"MIXED BAG OF EMOTIONS

Like a city whose walls are broken through is a person who lacks self-control(Proverbs 25:28 NIV)

Someone once asked to know what was going through my mind and what I was feeling at the time that I was going through what was the greatest challenge of my life. Well, that is why I decided to put pen to paper and talk about the emotional turmoil that ran me ragged. Emotionally, I was all over the place. This journey evoked a mixed bag of emotions within me. Our marriage was hanging by a thread; it had been shaken to the roots by this experience and the journey that had ensued as we were trying to have children.

We constantly worried about getting older and that we would never have children despite having everything else that packaged a "happy couple". It was an emotional roller coaster, but in all that turmoil, we rediscovered ourselves in Christ. Fear was a constant companion in that season. It gripped us and held us captive. In my frustration, I would question the whereabouts of this God who was not coming through for me. My wife had been going to church; my mother prayed for me; So where was their God? There was a lot of emotional pain which I would feel physically. I was angry. Angry with God. Angry with the world. I had never dabbled in crazy things, so why was this curse following me? I became angry with my wife and started blaming her for our lack of the fruit of the womb. It could not be my fault. Family and friends also added to this mixed bag of emotions. Their worry, their walking on eggshells around us and the pressure direct and indirect was overwhelming. Sometimes I felt that I was losing my mind and that I was going to have a major break down.

I remember that during the first two years of my marriage, I was not concerned about having children. We were intentionally not trying to have children. I was happy, confident, not worried and did not have a care in the world. We were so much in love and enjoying life. I thought that it would be that easy, decide and boom, we'd have children. When we eventually decided that it was time, nothing happened, and we started to take notice. I was getting stressed and very anxious. I began to worry and ask myself why I couldn't have children. "Was this it for me"? Time was moving and moving fast, and this got me thinking big time. Frustration started to rear its evil head, and the pressure got to me. I was now angry, at myself, my wife and the world. I was just so full of anger. I was arguing with and shouting at my wife and speaking hurtful words to her.

Fear and confusion consumed me, and I was starting to believe that it would never happen for us. My mind became the devil's playground at this time. Pride would rise and take over, convincing me that there could be nothing wrong with me. I would be overwhelmed by feelings of sadness as it became clear that my life was not perfect after all. I had no children, and yet everyone around me had children. I was scared. How would I move on? What if I never had children? What if I was the problem? What if she left me? I became depressed, and I was still in denial. Shame and disgrace were constant companions. I was now drinking alcohol heavily so that I could cope. I felt like giving up on everything, the marriage, trying for babies and life in general. I was not suicidal, but I wanted the pain to end.

Picture a mixed bag of assorted sweets, different types of candy, various shapes with different flavours. Some are bitter, some are sweet, and some are tangy; a bagful mixed with all sorts. They all carry within them a different taste. Now put this in the context of your emotions and imagine all your feelings in one bag. One minute you're sad, the next minute you're happy, and another minute you're on edge. Maybe the next minute you feel shame or even frustration and you want to give up. Imagine having no choice when you get the chance to pick that sweet in the mixed bag that you wish to and never knowing what you will come out with. When it came to how I felt, I never knew how I would feel from one day to the next.

Now ask me again, how did I feel? That was one question I hated because I had no idea how I'd be feeling from day to day. Some days were better than others. But one thing is for sure, knowing what I know now, I would rather feel this way and have this emotional turmoil with God in my life than without God. I know that with God even though I might be going through that emotional turbulence, I know that with Him there is hope, with God there is peace, and there is always light at the end of the tunnel. Even though I might walk through the valley, I will not fear anything for His rod, and His staff are always with me. (Psalm 23)

Without God, you wrestle with the confusion, the pain, the anger and all the other emotions, digging yourself into a deeper hole of despair. You react rather than respond. I encourage you to bring all your feelings to God. I trusted God that His word would make sense of all the emotional turmoil and turbulence that I was experiencing. The Bible says that "Do not be anxious or worried about anything, but in everything, every circumstance and situation, by prayer and petition with thanksgiving, continue to make your, specific, requests known to God. And the peace of God, that peace which reassures the heart, that peace, which transcends all understanding, that peace which, stands guard over your hearts and your minds in Christ Jesus, is yours" (Philippians4-6-7 AMP). With God, that mixed bag of emotions is not all that it's cut out to be. Hannah, amid her bitterness of the soul, was walking with God.

I want to encourage somebody that there is hope, and there is joy when you journey with God. When we make God the centre of our lives, His will and plans shall be done according to His word in the Bible. I remember that when I began to walk with God, things remained difficult and challenging as I did not see the result I wanted. I know that I had the word of God to reassure me, to bring me comfort, to give me peace, to build my faith and to provide me with that little bit of hope that I needed. I fell in love with this definition of hope when I was searching for the true meaning of hope. It said that "Christian hope is when God has promised that something is going to happen and you put your trust in that promise. Christian hope is a confidence that something will come to pass because God has promised it will come to pass". (Unknown). Hannah had hope, Abraham had hope, and I encourage you too to have that tenacious hope.

As men, we go through a myriad of emotions when we are faced with challenges in our lives. Our culture, religion, background and society all play a crucial role in how we manage and express these emotions. For the majority of the time, we don't manage them productively. Most times, we don't know how to handle the emotions; we don't know where to go for help or where to find a shoulder to cry on. Pride is the biggest hindrance. Where do we go for help spiritually and emotionally? It is hard being an emotionally chaotic man. Friends, family, professionals, religion were all within my reach, but making that first step was difficult. I took a chance on Jesus; I took a chance on the word of God when all seemed impossible.

Who are you reaching out to for that help? The pain is real; your tears are real. Start that journey of healing with just one step by reaching out. Those emotions are there, and they are not going anywhere. "Let not your heart be troubled; you believe in God, also believe in Me (John 14:1 NKJV). Take a chance with God.

CHAPTER 12

WHAT IF?

So humble yourselves under the mighty power of God, and at the right time, he will lift you up in honor. Give all your worries and cares to God, for he cares about you, (1Peter 5:6-7 NLT)

Sometimes You can't help but weigh the possibilities and probabilities of things working out. I engaged in this exercise many times the entire time that we believed God for children. Sometimes life throws so many lemons at you that knock you down, leaving you helpless with no clue as to how to turn them into lemonade. However much we may try to work things out, however much we may hope, sometimes there seems to be no relief to the pressures and storms that keep coming at you.

There are times that we will invest in prayer, times we will stand on the word of God and its promises for us believing with all that we have for answers, and all we may get is silence. The breakthrough we seek doesn't come through, and it may feel as if God is on the mute button. My wife and I waited ten long years for the blessing of the fruit of the womb. And yes, in the waiting season we questioned whether we would ever see the answers to our prayers. Yes, we did wonder if our faith was strong enough. So many times, I found myself asking the question, what if this God does not answer our prayers? Will I still believe in Him?

There are many other believers out there that wait for years and years and never see the answers to their prayers fulfilled. They never get to see what they desire happening in their lives come to pass. What happens then? What does one do? Is it the end of the world if you don't have children? What if it never happens? What does the bible say about not having children? Can you believe, have hope, have faith and still not have the fruit of the womb? Is that God saying no, or is it still within His will? Is Grace enough? What if...? This "What if" question was a springboard to many other questions that began to race around in my mind. What if it never happened? As believers, how do we cope with this reality? These are tough questions, but questions that reflect an everyday reality faced by believers. When you come face to face with such a seemingly immovable wall where do you run to? What fills your mind?

During the time we were believing for the fruit of the womb and getting to know God, I found myself delving into the bible in search of answers. I wanted to find out what God's word was concerning fruitfulness and what His promises were for those that were barren. I was driven by my obsession to have a child and not focusing on God Himself. The longer it took to get pregnant, the more time I spent in His word, reading and searching out His promises, His love and His assurances. I was trying to understand His plans, His purpose and His will for my life. I might not have understood what it was, but I was beginning to learn the nature of God. His word is full of promises for us; they are intended to build our faith and to keep us going.

There are many stories in the bible that display how God transformed a state of barrenness to fruitfulness. I clung onto these stories and scriptures for dear life. But the obsession with having children, that intense desire, above all else continued to haunt and drive me daily. I must add here that we should not allow this desire to overpower our relationship and understanding of who God is in our life. When in such a dark and seemingly hopeless place, it is very easy to fall into despair and self-condemnation. I encourage anyone facing such a challenge not to give up on God but to go back to basics. Go back to the foundations of who God is and what He stands for, who He is and what He has said to you and about you. What are His thoughts towards you, and what has He said about that wall that stands before you?

I encourage you to believe and trust that He loves you and has your best interests at heart. We know that God is Love. We know that He is concerned about everything that concerns us. We know that He forgives. We know that He is a good Father. His word stands true and is unchangeable. He is not fickle as we are therefore we must understand that the way He maps our lives out may sometimes be different to how we want to see our lives mapped out. "For My thoughts are not your thoughts, nor are your ways My ways," says the Lord. "For as the heavens are higher than the earth, So are My ways higher than your ways, And My thoughts than your thoughts (Isaiah 55:8-9 NKJV).

God, in His infinite wisdom, knows what is right for us at any given time. And when we accept this truth, we must learn to always pray "according to His will" and according to His time. And then wait. I do not profess to say that this will be an easy road to walk, but all we have to hold on to is our faith. And God responds to faith. When we offer Him our faith, He promises not to leave us alone in our pain. There are many things that we may never understand about our God until we meet face to face with Him, and one of these may be why some of our prayers were never answered. There will be so many questions that we may never know the answers to until we come face to face with our Maker.

Understand first and foremost that it is not your fault that you are facing infertility. It is not because you lack faith or that you are a terrible sinner. We need to close our ears to what the world says and focus on what the word of God says. Focus on who God is and what He says about your life. The Bible is full of men and women who faced and lived with their challenges. The Apostle Paul, a man full of faith, preaching the word with power and moving in signs and wonders, had to face life with an affliction that did not leave his body even after crying out to God for healing. God gave him an answer that we need to understand and learn from and live by. "And He said to me, "My grace is sufficient for you, for My strength is made perfect in weakness" (2 Corinthians 12:9 NKJV). The thorn in Paul's flesh did not go away because God had a purpose in not removing it.

God can deal with barrenness or infertility. It's not new to Him. It is not so impossible that He cannot deal with it. It's not news to Him that you are walking this journey. What we know and must hold on to is His word, which promises that He works everything out for our good and that His grace will always be sufficient for us. Ultimately everything He does is good because He is not the author of evil or wickedness.

In the Bible, we encounter many women of God who had to deal with barrenness. Sarah, Abram's wife, had no child well into her 90s. The Bible says that she was barren. Rebekkah, Isaac's wife, was barren. Hannah had no children. Rachel was barren. Elizabeth was well into her advanced age with no children. These were all Godly women whom God used to be part of the lineage that would bring forth the Messiah, Jesus Christ. God has His ways that only He knows about. Only He knows how He will bring about His purposes in our lives. Only He can turn our barrenness into fruitfulness. Only He can transform any desert places in our lives into an oasis. But most times, before that can happen, there may be a process and a journey to be walked through before He reveals His plans. There may be certain things in our lives that He needs to deal with before entrusting us with the abundance and overflow of His blessings.

Nowhere in the Bible does God condemn or speak negatively against infertile or barren women who never have or will never give birth. The Bible says "He makes the barren woman be a homemaker and a joyful mother of [spiritual] children". Praise the Lord, (Psalm 113:9 AMPC). Sometimes God chooses a path for us to walk that will be uncomfortable. But He knows the plans, purpose, and will for our lives. The will of God for our life is good. "In Christ, we too have been claimed as God's possession, since we were predestined according to the one purpose of him who accomplishes all things according to the counsel of his will". (Ephesians 1:11 NET), "Be thankful in all circumstances, for this is God's will for you who belong to Christ Jesus. (1 Thessalonians 5:18 NLT). "You need to persevere so that when you have done the will of God, you will receive what he has promised". (Hebrews 10:36 NIV).

The will of God is never easy because we do not understand it, nor do we fully understand His nature. The bible says "Seek the Kingdom of God above all else, and live righteously, and he will give you everything you need". (Matthew 6:33 NLT). Be intentional about knowing God more, having a relationship with Him, understanding that it is about His will and not your will. The amplified version of the same scripture reads "But first and most importantly seek, (aim at, strive after), His kingdom and His righteousness [His way of doing and being right-the attitude and character of God], and all these things will be given to you also". All things like peace, gratitude and the lack of worry will be yours. You will experience the manifestation of His Word and His will in your life.

I pray that this difficult chapter has stirred something in you. May the will of God for your life prevail and manifest itself for you.

CHAPTER 13

LOST WITHOUT YOU

He who finds a [true and faithful] wife finds a good thing And obtains favour and approval from the Lord".
(Proverbs 18:22 AMP).

"I'm so sorry, but your wife has been in a serious car accident," said the voice at the other end of the phone. I did not understand. How could this be? I'd just seen her off to work a few minutes ago. I was freaking out, and tears were running down my face. All I could think of was that I could not live without her; what will I do without her? What am I going to tell her mother? Why me God? The shock hit me, and I could not think straight. We had so many things going on with the challenges of trying for a baby and now this? When you are going through a difficult season in your life, you may find yourself dodging a few curveballs.

My father's voice penetrated through the haze of confusion, asking me what the matter was; why was I crying? I was completely frozen, numb with shock. Then panic took over, and I needed to get out and get to her quickly. My parents were trying to calm me down, but I was not to be calmed. My dad accompanied me to the accident scene, and when we got there, my wife was seated in the ambulance. I rushed over to her and broke down, crying. The shock was too much for me. The police reported that she had been fortunate to come out alive, and that was down to the car that she drove, which had a solid body. The car was an old 1995 BMW 3 series. Had she been driving any of the newer cars, they would not have been able to handle the impact so well. My wife would have perished at the scene. I was so thankful that her life had been spared. This accident woke me right up. It was a harsh and painful wake-up call. Always give thanks and appreciate what you have.

The accident took place well before we had the children while we were still believing and fighting off despair and disappointment. This incident was crucial in helping me to put things into their proper perspective. It happened just before we started our journey of getting to know God and being a part of the Kingdom Church family. At that point, I realised that all other things were unimportant if I did not have my wife beside me. We had wasted so much time fighting over meaningless things that did not add any value to our lives; instead, they stole precious time from us and what we could do together. I realised there and then that I could easily have lost her and I would have been utterly lost and bereft without her. My life would have had no meaning. There would be no reason for me to continue living. God has now shown me through His word that "Whatever is good and perfect is a gift coming down to us from God our Father, who created all the lights in the heavens. He never changes or casts a shifting shadow" (James 1:17 NLT).

Whatever problems or challenges the devil tries to pile on, trust God that He has your back. The more you fear, the more it comes to pass. Job said that what he greatly feared the most had come to pass. He lost what was important to him because of fear. Never be afraid. My encouragement to you is never to let the devil make you live in fear. Have faith that God will see you through every challenge. Have faith that God will lift you. Fear opens up an opportunity for the enemy to work against you. You will not lose anything; you will not lose your relationship; you will not lose your marriage, your husband or your wife in the name of Jesus. You will not lose your God-given gift.

After all has been said and done, during the storms and the fires, the despair and the anger, some things will stand out as being of utmost priority. I am a man that was utterly lost, walking blindly in the wilderness with absolutely no direction. My life would not be the same if it were not for this one person in my life. I would not be who I am today, a husband, a father and a man of God had it not been for her. I, therefore, give thanks to God for giving me a wonderful and able helper. A woman of substance and wisdom. I thank God that my wife is a loving mother to my children. She is my intercessor and my friend. She holds our home together, calmly and peacefully. Would I be who I am today were she not in my life? I think not, for she has played such a crucial part in guiding and speaking into my life. Would I have had my three miracles today that I call Samuel, David and Taome without her? I think not. I would be lost without her. I cherish my wife, and we continue to grow in love and Christ together.

Today I want to encourage you. Give God the glory for your wife, give God the glory for your husband. Fear should never be your portion. Together you can overcome adversity. Let God be the centre of your relationship. A person standing alone can be attacked and defeated, but two can stand back-to-back and conquer. Three are even better, for a triple-braided cord is not easily broken. (Ecclesiastes 4:12 NLT). My wife remains my strength to succeed; she continues to nurture the desires in me; she has made our house a home and has made our life something out of nothing. I dedicate this chapter to pay a special tribute to my wife, who stood strong with me through it all. "You are altogether beautiful, my darling; there is no flaw in you". (Song of Songs 4:7 NIV).

CHAPTER 14

FEROCIOUS TENACITY

I love the story of Hannah in the Bible, found in 1 Samuel 1. It chronicles the birth of Samuel. In this story, I see a woman who had ferocious tenacity during a time when what she desired most appeared to be impossible. The odds looked as though they were against her, but she continued to worship God amid the disappointment.

My question to you is, what are you doing in your season of discouragement and despair? I know it's easier said than done, and that is why I want to encourage someone to let go and let God be God. When you read about Hannah, you begin to see and learn that she is not that different from you and what you are going through. Hannah also felt what you feel, the lost hope, the anger, the disgrace and feeling unloved. Her life on the outside appeared amazing; she was married; she had her own home and had a husband who feared God. What more could she have asked for? But the challenges of life know no race nor gender, and her life which appeared perfect began to show the cracks. Her pain was real. She had no children, and the Bible tells us that was because the Lord had left her childless.

Sometimes you too might feel like Hannah; that God has forgotten you, that God does not love you or pay attention to you and what matters to you. You too feel the pain, the hurt, confusion and rejection. Yes, Hannah experienced it all. Despite all the pain, Hannah continued seeking the face of God; going to church without fail, despite the disgrace and mockery she received from Peninah, which resulted in the bitterness of the soul. The Bible tells us that when King David was downcast and discouraged, he encouraged himself in the lord. (1Samuel 30). Hannah too continued to encourage herself in God, and so should you. She never tired or gave up worshipping God, despite not seeing a breakthrough. Her ability to hold on is a clear reflection of her relationship with God, which was rooted and grounded on His will. I say to you today, be grounded and rooted in God and His will for your life. She was human, and she let it show as she would cry out to God. It is never easy, but you too can cry unto the Lord.

The children of Israel cried bitterly unto the Lord when the Egyptians oppressed them. The Lord God heard their cry. I want to encourage someone that the Lord God has heard your cry. It took one day for Hannah's life to change. It took one day for my life to change and I want to tell you that it will take one day for your life to change. There are two things I picked up from the story of Hannah; that it is about the will of God and that it also takes you playing your part. Hannah made up her mind to remain focused on God and His promises despite the pain of not seeing the fruit that she sought. I was lost, down and out. Going through the pain and emotional turmoil without God was agony. Before I knew God, I was comforted by false narratives and used alcohol to numb my feelings and yet found no peace. When I made up my mind to know God as my Father, though the emotional turmoil was still there, I was comforted by Him and His word. Suddenly there was peace and hope in the midst of chaos.

Hannah has a ferocious tenacity about her. The Bible tells us that "It came about in due time, after Hannah had conceived, that she gave birth to a son; she named him Samuel, saying, "Because I have asked for him from the Lord", (1 Samuel 1:20 AMP). Today surrender and trust God, you will be pregnant with your joy, with your breakthrough and with your miracle. You will birth your Samuel, you will testify about the goodness of God. It was not easy for me, but I began the journey. I want to encourage you to begin the journey today, no matter what and how you are feeling. Your breakthrough starts today.

As I continued to read the story of Hannah, I began to draw some lessons from it. There is power in the spoken word of God, which we saw when Hannah repeatedly sought and spoke the word of God into her situation. I believe that she was confessing fruitfulness over her situation. You, too, can hold onto the powerful word of God. Speak something different; confession and affirmation will bring you manifestation. "So shall my word be that goeth forth out of my mouth: it shall not return unto me void, but it shall accomplish that which I please, and it shall prosper in the thing whereto I sent it". (Isaiah 55:11, KJV).

There is a hidden enemy of progress that can make you focus on the wrong things. That enemy is yourself. Hannah would be provoked and end up reacting by crying and not eating hence losing focus on the plans and purpose of God. When she focused on God and her breakthrough, something amazing happened. Focus on your Samuel and the will of God for your life. The enemy from within which is represented by your soul or emotions can distract you from your destiny. This enemy from within can destroy your faith, trust and hope in God and what He can do for you.

Don't foster frustration, hate or any negative emotions that can block your breakthrough. "Then Elkanah her husband said to her, "Hannah, why do you weep? Why do you not eat? And why is your heart grieved? Am I not better to you than ten sons?" (1Samuel 1:8 NKJV). You can cry to God with regards to your situation. Year after year, month after month, day after day, I believe that Hannah cried unto the Lord that He might hear her, and bring about her breakthrough. I began to see that when you cry unto God, He does hear you. In the book of Exodus, the children of Israel cried unto God when the Egyptians oppressed them. Never be ashamed to cry to God. He will hear you. Be consistent and persistent. Hannah stayed true and always went to the house of God year after year despite the challenges of being barren. You might not see the answer or the result or the outcome of your prayer, but I want to encourage you to remain persistent, be consistent, and you will see the goodness of God.

When you begin to see what Hannah went through, you begin to see that she had ferocious tenacity. She was human, but her actions showed that she had hope even though it was against the odds. She never gave up. When you look at the word ferocious, it means vicious, extreme or being intense. It is identified with aggressiveness. When you look at the word tenacity, it means being persistent or relentless about something. Hannah's nature brought out that ferocious tenacity within her; for Hannah ferocious tenacity meant never giving up, being bold, being courageous amid the barrenness. She made up her mind that despite the storm, she was going to ride the waves. And this is what you need today as you are going through your journey; you need that ferocious tenacity.

CHAPTER 15

LESSONS TO DRAW FROM THIS BOOK

BE FEROCIOUS ABOUT GOD

As you seek to know God more and to understand the significance of what Jesus did for you, I encourage you to be faithful, to remain loyal and steadfast in trusting and believing in God without wavering. With God, all things are possible. His plans, His purpose and His will are His goodness for your life. "So don't worry about these things, saying, 'What will we eat? What will we drink? What will we wear?' These things dominate the thoughts of unbelievers, but your heavenly Father already knows all your needs. Seek the Kingdom of God above all else, and live righteously, and he will give you everything you need". (Matthew 6:31-33 NLT). It's in God's hands.

BE FEROCIOUS IN FAITH

Faith means believing the word of God wholeheartedly. Faith believes that whatever the word of God says about your situation is correct. The bible states that as you hear the word of God regularly, your faith increases (Romans10:27). Abraham was facing a seemingly impossible situation where he believed God for a child and waited 25 years to see the promise come to fulfilment. But he believed, he had faith that God would do it. Though he went on to have Ismael, God reassured him that he would still have the promised child, he remained steadfast in his faith. I urge you to continue to build and grow in your faith.

BE FEROCIOUS IN PRAYER.

When you are facing a wall, something has to give. Be consistent and persistent in prayer. The Bible tells us in Luke18:1 and 1Thessalonians 5:1 that we must pray always. Pray when you feel like praying, pray when you don't feel like praying, in and out of season. There is something that happens when you pray. "Therefore, confess your sins to one another [your false steps, your offences], and pray for one another, that you may be healed and restored. The heartfelt and persistent prayer of a righteous man (believer) can accomplish much [when put into action and made effective by God-it is dynamic and can have tremendous power]", (James 5:16 AMP). There is power in prayer.

BE FEROCIOUS IN YOUR CRY UNTO GOD

The children of Israel cried to God when the Egyptians oppressed them. God heard their cry and moved mightily, delivering them from the hand of oppression. Many people in the Bible cried out to God. King Hezekiah cried to God when the Prophet Isaiah told him he would die. The church in the book of Acts cried unto God when Peter was jailed. Never be afraid to cry to God about your problem. "Hear my cry, O God; Attend to my prayer". (Psalm 61:1 NKJV). God will hear your cry from heaven.

BE FEROCIOUS IN YOUR TRUST IN GOD

It is of paramount importance that you trust God with all your might in your walk with him. As a man, it can be hard to put your trust in something you have no control over. Sometimes when your five human senses struggle to make sense of situations, it is hard to trust. But God and His word can transform your life. When you let go and let God be God, when you trust and believe Him, He will show you His power and love. "Trust in the LORD with all your heart; do not depend on your understanding" (Proverbs 3:5 NLT).

BE FEROCIOUS IN BELIEVING HIS PROMISES

When you begin to trust and walk with God, you will see the promises that are stored in His word. God is faithful to His promises. Sometimes we experience a delay, and we think it is denial. God kept His promise to Abraham and Sarah with regards to having their child. Trust and believe that God will fulfil His promises to you. "Let us hold tightly without wavering to the hope we affirm, for God can be trusted to keep his promise", (Hebrews 10:23 NLT). Be ferocious in your desire and hopes that Gods promises will manifest in your life.

BE FEROCIOUS IN ACCEPTING THAT
HIS WILL SHALL BE DONE IN YOUR LIFE

The will of God for your life is always good. Trust that His will is going to manifest in your life. Understand what His word in the Bible promises you according to His will. "Now this is the confidence that we have in Him, that if we ask anything according to His will, He hears us. And if we know that He hears us, whatever we ask, we know that we have the petitions that we have asked of Him", (1John 5:14-15 NKJV). Have faith and remain ferocious in your hope that it shall come to pass.

BE FEROCIOUS ABOUT WAITING UPON THE LORD

Waiting is one of the most difficult things that we have to deal with. Hannah, Abraham, Rebecca all went through the journey of waiting for the fruit of the womb. They experienced the uncertainty of believing that what you can't feel or see will come to pass. God's word is full of testimonies on the power of waiting and trusting the Lord. "Yet I am confident I will see the LORD's goodness while I am here in the land of the living. Wait patiently for the LORD. Be brave and courageous. Yes, wait patiently for the LORD", (Psalm 27:13-14 NLT). Waiting on the Lord demonstrates trusting in God's goodness and timing.

PRAYER

"Now Jesus was telling the disciples a parable to make the point that at all times they ought to pray and not give up and lose heart". (Luke18:1 AMP).

After I finished writing this book, I went back to read it, and it allowed me to relive my journey quite vividly. I felt all the emotions as before, the pain, the fear, the joy and everything that I had gone through during that season. I can testify that prayer is what held me down and kept me going so that I was able to come out the other end stronger, to the glory of God. With God, all things are possible. I want to pray for you because prayer brought me peace and allowed me to continue through my season of barrenness. May God hear your cry today in the name of Jesus.

LET US PRAY

Heavenly Father I come humbly before your throne of grace today. You alone are the Most High God. Your name is Jehovah, the one who heals, the one who remembers and the one who brings joy and peace to all. Today I lift my voice in prayer as I cry out unto you, Lord, for your sons and daughters that are going through a season of barrenness in their households.

Father, I ask that you give them the strength to walk this journey with you in the name of Jesus. I take authority and come against every pain, against every worry, against every fear, against every depression, against every frustration, against every shame, against every disgrace and against any thoughts of giving up. I reject every emotional turmoil in their life that is bringing confusion and thoughts against the gift of life. Today I speak peace over their minds, peace over their marriages and peace over every turmoil that the spirit of barrenness is bringing into their life. May your grace be sufficient for them as they walk this challenging journey. I believe and receive that your will shall be done over their situation in Jesus Mighty Name.

Today I declare and decree that the yoke of barrenness is broken, I declare and decree that you are released. May the fruit of thy womb be blessed, may it bring you joy, may it bring you peace and may it bring you comfort in the name of Jesus. May the will of God reign over your life. I thank you, Heavenly Father, for I know that you have heard our prayer in the name of Jesus.

Amen.

Printed in Great Britain
by Amazon

28891871R00056